Precious Metal Clay In Mixed Media

Bringing It All Together

by Mary Ann Devos

Wardell
PUBLICATIONS INC

Special Thanks From The Author

The inspiration and support for this book have come from many sources. I have learned so much from watching my students approach this magical clay material. Sharing the process with you has helped me to further develop these techniques. I wish I could list all of you.

- A special thanks goes to Tim McCreight, Consultant for Mitsubishi Materials Corporation, my first PMC teacher.

- Thank you also to CeCe Wire, Administrator of the PMC Guild, for her continued support.

- I wish to express my gratitude to Earl Roberts, manager of PMC Connection and president of Sierra Thermal Industries, Inc., manufacturer of Sierra kilns. He is a great business partner and has encouraged me since the beginning of my silver clay career. I am proud to be the Director of Education for PMC Connection and to work with such a progressive, innovative team.

- Thanks to Mr. Masao Hoshide, President of Mikuni American, Inc. for his support of PMC Connection.

- Thanks to Mr. Dennis Nakashima, Vice President of Mikuni American, Inc. for all his kindness and guidance.

- I wish to thank Mr. Akira Nishio, Vice General Manager and Mr. Atsushi Nishiyama, Assistant Manager of the Advanced Products Company of Mitsubishi Materials Corporation of Japan. They have been very generous and encouraging.

- I thank Mr. Eisuke Kojima and Mr. Daisuke Kojima, of SunArt, for helping to facilitate our bi-cultural connection.

- All of the Senior Teachers of the PMC Connection are a joy to share this experience with. They are a dynamic teaching team.

- Thanks to those who contributed to this book: Linda Bernstein, Sondra Busch, Mary Ellin D'Agostino, Tonya Davidson, Sherry Fotopoulos, Patti Genack, Vera Lightstone, Hattie Sanderson, Marlynda Taylor, Helen & Dick Tickal and Leslie Tieke.

- A book like this would not be possible without the wonderful art direction and editing skills of my publisher Randy Wardell.

- Ken Devos, my husband, has provided a tremendous amount of support for all my traveling, teaching and book writing. He offers computer, editorial and emotional support to all our endeavors and I appreciate him greatly.

> Notice: Due to variable conditions, materials and user skill levels, the publisher, author and material manufacturers disclaim any liability for adverse reaction, injury or loss resulting from the use of information in this publication.
>
> Trade named tools and products, manufactured materials and/or proprietary processes mentioned or photographed for this publication are Trademarked™ and Copyrighted© by the respective manufacturers. All rights reserved.

Precious Metal Clay In Mixed Media is Copyright© 2007 by Wardell Publications Inc

Precious Metal Clay In Mixed Media original printing was Publiahed & Copyright© 2004 by Wardell Publications Inc

Precious Metal Clay In Mixed Media is exclusively published by Wardell Publications, Inc. ALL RIGHTS RESERVED. Copyright© 2007 Mary Ann Devos. No part of this publication may be reproduced or used for any reason or by any means, whether graphic, electronic, or mechanical, including photocopying, digital scanning, recording, taping, or information storage & retrieval systems or otherwise, without the prior permission in writing from the publisher.

The text, layout and designs of this book, as well as the book in its entirety, are protected by the copyright laws of the United States (17 U.S.C. 101 et seq.) and similar laws in other countries.

Wardell Publications Inc. in partnership with the Author & Designer, Mary Ann Devos, grants limited permission to produce a work(s) from the designs contained in this book, for personal use only (not for commercial resale), provided that the production quantity does not exceed more than one (1) unit derived from any design contained herein. This permission does not extend to the reproduction or reprinting, whether re-drawn, enlarged or otherwise altered, for distribution or any other use, of any pattern, drawing, photograph, or text contained in this book, or of the book as a whole.

Commercial production of works based in part or in whole upon the designs contained in this book is strictly forbidden without the prior written permission of the publisher. Please consult the copyright section of our website http://www.wardellpublications.com for information on how to obtain permission to produce a work(s) from any book, pattern or design published by Wardell Publications Inc. and offer it for commercial resale.

Cataloguing in Publication Data
Mary Ann Devos,
  Precious Metal Clay In Mixed Media: Bringing It All Together / author: Mary Ann Devos; senior editor Ken Devos
  Includes Index
  ISBN-13: 978-0-919985-43-8
  ISBN-10: 0-919985-43-2
  1. Jewelry making 2. Precious Metal Clay
  1. Devos, Ken II. Title.
  TT213.D495 2004   739.2   C2004-904005-7

Printed in Thailand by Phongwarin Printing Ltd.
Published simultaneously in Canada and USA
E-mail: info@wardellpublications.com
Website: www.wardellpublications.com

Precious Metal Clay In Mixed Media
Bringing It All Together

Author: Mary Ann Devos
Senior Editor: Ken Devos
Jewelry Design & Fabrication by:
Contributing Artists (see page 94)
Text Editor: Randy Wardell

Photography: Ken Devos and
Rob Stegmann (except as noted on photos)
Layout & Design: Randy Wardell
Art Assistance: Esteban Luna
Cover Design: Christine Arleij

Dedication: To our next generation: Christy, Shawn, Kim & Lance

Published by

Send your comments and suggestions or sign-up to receive our "New Editions" digital newsletter.
Contact us by E-mail: info@wardellpublications.com or visit our Website at: www.wardellpublications.com

Author / Designer: Mary Ann Devos
Editor & Photographer: Ken Devos

Mary Ann Devos, "Pearl in a Wave"
Photo: Rob Stegmann

Author Notes

A note from Mary Ann Devos

Precious Metal Clay (PMC) combines the playfulness of clay with the value and permanence of pure silver and gold. It is easy to work with and fun. As you enjoy creating with it you make heirloom quality jewelry or sculpture.

This material is manufactured by Mitsubishi Materials Corporation and is available in fine silver (.999) and 22K gold. It is composed of microscopic particles of precious metal, a non-toxic organic binder and water. It looks, feels and is shaped very similar to potter's clay but when it's fired all that is left is solid precious metal.

During my 25 year career as an RN, I worked as a nursing administrator and teacher. My BS degree in management has been a valuable tool both as a nurse and as an artist. I spent much of my leisure time as a mixed media artist in pottery, stained glass, fabric and metals. I have worked as a full-time artist since 1995.

I have used PMC since 1996 when it was introduced to the USA market. As Director of Education for PMC Connection, part of the PMC Guild USA, it has been my privilege to write the certification program for the PMC Connection track. The projects for the Level 1 Certification class are covered in my first book, *Introduction To Precious Metal Clay*.

For this new book I created projects that build upon the techniques presented in our first book. In addition, some of the PMC Connection Senior Teachers, accomplished artists all, have shared their favorite projects with us. These teachers are a great group to work with. Their creative energy is overwhelming.

It has been a joy to travel around the world and throughout the USA introducing people to this wonderful new medium and I have had the privilege to teach in Japan, Europe, Canada and very soon in other countries as well.

The focus of this book is PMC used in combination with a wide range of other materials. The projects are influenced by the global art of Mother Earth.

The range of the projects presented here demonstrates that with PMC you are limited only by your imagination. Every day we discover new ways to create with PMC. Whether you are a jeweler, polymer, ceramic, fabric, glass or doll artist, this material can enrich your work. I hope that you enjoy our efforts and find some interesting things to spark your own creativity.

A note from Ken Devos

For much of my life I have worked in a wide range of artistic media including creative photography, woodworking and fiber arts. In 1989 I turned my attention to working in metals, concentrating in hand made silver chains and intricate techniques using metals in textile processes. Since the mid 1990's I have been involved with the use and marketing of silver clay and currently I am Program Coordinator for PMC Connection. I have enjoyed sharing my experience of working with this magical material, it is my hope that it becomes as important to you as it has been for me.

Author Contact Information

Mary Ann & Ken Devos
Phone: (239) 463-8006
Email: pmcconnection@aol.com
Website: www.silverclayworks.com

Table Of Contents — Page

- Introduction to Precious Metal Clay 6
- The Many Forms of Precious Metal Clay 6
- Firing Chart 8
- Safety First - How to Keep it Fun 9
- Tools, Equipment & Kilns 10

Fundamental Techniques

- Forming, Shaping and Texturing 15
- Gemstones, Findings and Mountings 17
- Drying, Refining and Firing 19
- Finishing, Polishing and Antiquing 22

The Projects

- **Gallery**   PMC Bead Garden 25
- **Chapter 1**   PMC and Glass Gallery .... 26 & 27
    - Garnish Dish 28
    - Dichroic Glass and Fine Silver Brooch 30
    - Silver Painting on Glass 32
- **Chapter 2**   PMC and Enamel 'On' Gallery .... 34 - 36
    - Moonstar Pendant 37
- **Gallery**   PMC and Enamel 'In' Gallery 39
    - Wave Earrings 40
- **Chapter 3**   PMC and Polymer Clay Gallery ...... 42 & 43
    - Polymer Clay Art Earrings 44
- **Chapter 4**   PMC Silver and Gold Gallery .... 46 & 47
    - Gold Paste Highlights on Silver Pendant 48
    - Gold Clay Stamped Earrings 50
    - Keum Boo, Gold Foil Technique 52
- **Chapter 5**   PMC and Ceramics Gallery 54
    - Decorating Fine Porcelain Dolls 56
    - Silver Coated Ceramic Beads 58
    - Stoneware Plate with Silver Figure 60
- **Chapter 6**   PMC Carved and Punched Gallery .. 62 & 63
    - Carved In Silver 64
    - Sheet Clay Pendants And Earrings 66
- **Chapter 7**   PMC and Mixed Metals Gallery ...... 68 & 69
    - Bones & Stones Necklace Pendant 70
    - Rain Dancer Wire Figure 72
    - Chain Mail Bracelet 74
    - Fibula Pin 77
- **Chapter 8**   PMC and Sculptural Forms Gallery .. 78 & 79
    - Birds Nest Sculpture - The Next Generation 80
    - Silver Box with Hinged Lid 82
    - Sculptural Rings 86
    - Turning Nature Into Silver 88
- **Chapter 9**   Trouble Shooting Questions and Answers .... 92 & 93

- Contributing Artist Instructor Bio's 94
- Index 95

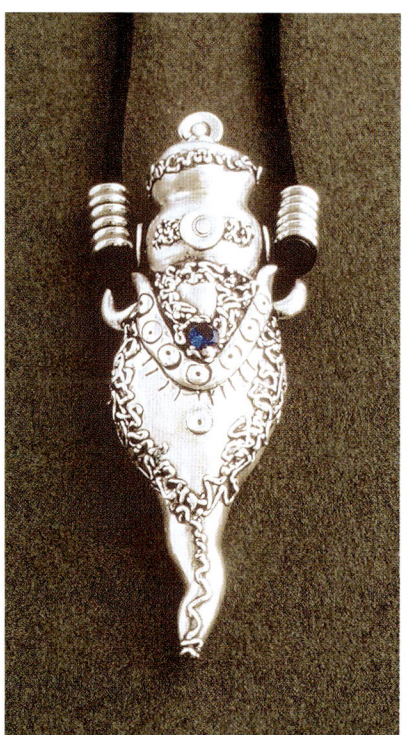

Hattie Sanderson, "Potion Vessel"
Photo: Hattie Sanderson

Sherry Fotopoulos, "Kimono Pin"
Photo: Rob Stegmann

Bringing It All Together

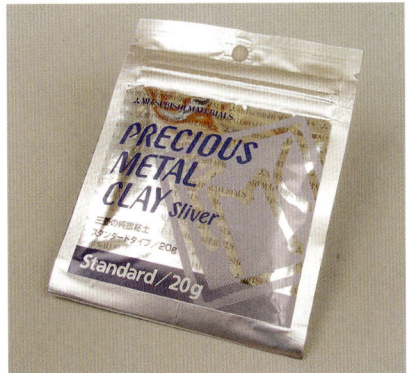

PMC Standard in lump form

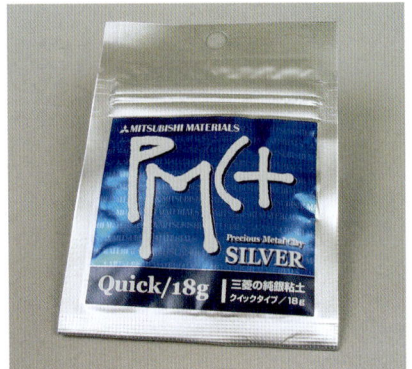

PMC+ in resealable foil bag

PMC3 in resealable foil bag

PMC 22K Gold in lump form

Introduction to Precious Metal Clay

Precious Metal Clay (also called 'PMC') was developed in the early 1990's by Mitsubishi Materials Corporation of Japan. It is composed of micron sized particles of precious metal, a non-toxic organic binder and water and is available in fine silver (.999) and 22K gold. It didn't take long for this product to be recognized as a unique material for jewelry making. Its clay-like qualities allow artists to manipulate and shape it using basic, uncomplicated tools. The dried clay art piece is transformed by firing it in a small tabletop kiln, to burn off the binder and fuse the metal particles together, revealing a pure precious metal object. You will find it difficult to contain your enthusiasm the first time you experience this magical process. Once you have recognized the vast potential, your creative instincts will bring on a flood of possibilities.

The Many Forms of Precious Metal Clay

PMC is available in three slightly different silver formulas. PMC Standard, PMC+ and PMC3 in addition to the PMC 22K Gold. Each product is composed of powdered precious metals, (fine silver or gold), a non-toxic organic binder (the clay-like substrate) and water. The primary differences among the three silver materials are the firing times, firing temperatures and shrinkage rates. Each of these factors is a result of the differences in the metal particle sizes and the percentages of binder in the clay. These differences plus other distinctive working characteristics will influence the type and style of jewelry pieces that you will make.

Precious Metal Clay - Product Types

PMC Standard:

This product is available in lump-clay format only and is also the most economical of all the PMC materials. It can be rolled into sheets, pinch formed, roll-coiled and hand molded into a great variety of personal adornments. This original formula material consists of slightly larger particles and it contains a higher percentage of binder material and water, as compared to the other PMC products. As a result, this material stays moist and workable for a longer period and is less prone to cracking during the drying stage. It will shrink approximately 30% from the wet or moldable state to the finished fired stage. This can be used to advantage on highly detailed pieces as the shrinking actually intensifies the surface texture and detail. The larger metal particles also result in a more porous, less dense and therefore a lighter-weight finished object. However this porous quality also means it's not as strong and should not be used for items that will be subjected to a lot of wear and tear. In addition, due to the higher firing temperature and longer firing time, fused glass components are not recommended but lab-grown stones fire well with this clay form. As with all PMC the fired pieces are solid pure silver.

PMC+:

The development of this clay formula brought many breakthrough advantages to metal clay artists. The metal particles are much smaller as compared to PMC Standard and are therefore more densely packed. The result is a stronger finished piece that only shrinks about 12% from the moldable stage making it better suited for higher wear items like rings and bracelets. Since the shrinkage is smaller and measurable, it is easier to make rings and other items that must be precisely sized. PMC+ works well in combination with enamels, ceramic and most lab-grown gemstones. Due to the short firing time, you can fire PMC+ with a small butane torch. The fired pieces are solid pure silver (.999).

PMC3:

This clay formula is a further advancement in the PMC line-up. It has the same basic working characteristics as PMC+ but fires at an even lower temperature. PMC3 can be used in combination with the same media as PMC+ however the lower temperature schedule makes it ideal to use with some natural gemstones. Sterling silver findings can be added during fabrication and fired without weakening the structure of the sterling components. PMC3 is the clay type always recommended for use with glass. Finally PMC3 can be fired using a butane torch and other inexpensive kilns, opening up a whole world of new possibilities.

PMC Gold:

PMC Gold clay is currently available in lump form only but research is underway with plans to introduce other formats in the near future. Originally available as 24 K, the current gold clay is 22 K, an alloy of 24 K gold and .999 silver (91.6% gold and 8.4% silver). As with all PMC forms, PMC Gold models and takes textures in exactly the same way as the silver clay. The metal particle size and working properties are similar to PMC Plus and it also shrinks about 14-19% after firing. PMC Gold has a firing temperature very similar to PMC+ with a firing time of 10 to 90 minutes. It is possible to use both gold and silver PMC in the same project, firing them both in a single step. To insure a secure connection between the two metals, construct the silver to capture the gold component. Another technique is to make a gold paste by adding distilled water to the gold clay, applying the paste over dried but unfired PMC+ or PMC3 and torch firing the combined metals.

Sondra Busch, "Folded Leaves" Pendant, Photo: Rob Stegmann

Mary Ann Devos, "Donora Bead" Stamped silver clay with syringe clay edges and 22K gold PMC paste, Photo: Ken Devos

Elissa Cossey, "Barrel Bead"
Photo: Ken Devos

Important Note

To achieve maximum strength, all types of PMC silver can be fired at 1650°F/900°C for 2 hours. However, if the fabricated item has inclusions you must make an allowance in the firing schedule for the specific requirement of the inclusion (see page 21).

Lump clay type, soft and moldable right out of the package.

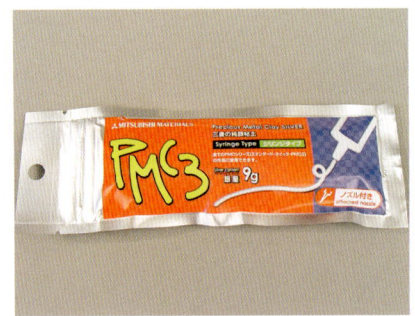

Syringe clay type

Precious Metal Clay Firing Chart

The following chart compares the firing schedules and shrinkage for all PMC types in both silver and 22K gold.

Product Type	Firing Temperature	Firing Time	Shrinkage
PMC Standard	1650°F / 900°C	2 hours	30%
PMC+	1650°F / 900°C	10 minutes	12%
PMC+	1560°F / 850°C	20 minutes	12%
PMC+	1470°F / 800°C	30 minutes	12%
PMC3	1290°F / 700°C	10 minutes	12%
PMC3	1200°F / 650°C	20 minutes	12%
PMC3	1110°F / 600°C	45 minutes	12%
PMC 22K Gold	1650°F / 900°C	10 minutes	14% to 19%
PMC 22K Gold	1560°F / 850°C	30 minutes	14% to 19%
PMC 22K Gold	1380°F / 750°C	60 minutes	14% to 19%
PMC 22K Gold	1290°F / 700°C	90 minutes	14% to 19%

Metal Clay Product Formats

All PMC clay formulas are available in the lump form but there are several other formats that enhance the experience of working with this amazing material. Remember, pieces made from these products will be solid, pure precious metal, either fine silver (.999) or pure gold (22K) after firing.

Lump Clay:

All PMC clay formulas are available in this most versatile of all format compositions. This lump clay type can be slab rolled, pinched, coiled, molded, textured, cut, ripped and shaped in just about any way you can possibly imagine. Right out of the package it is the consistency of children's modeling clay. However it will quickly begin to dry out and become more difficult to mold and shape. It is important to keep all unused portions sealed away in plastic wrap and to continually dampen your working form to keep it hydrated until you are satisfied with the final shape.

Syringe Clay:

PMC+ and PMC3 are available already loaded into a syringe type applicator. Syringe Clay can be used alone or in combination with any of the other material formats. This very soft clay is extruded through the syringe nozzle to form a delicate string that can be used for many things from simple repairs to drawing fanciful filigree designs. It is often used to embellish the surface of lump-clay or paste clay work and is a great way to form custom bezels for stone settings. Many artists use it to decorate porcelain, hand built pottery, contemporary ceramics or porcelain dolls.

Paste Clay:

PMC+ and PMC3 products are mixed to the consistency of white glue and packaged in small jars. Sometimes referred to as 'slip', it is normally applied with a small artist's paintbrush. It is most often used as a glue to help assemble lump-clay pieces. It can fill and smooth edges and joints and will fill any cracks or blemishes in your piece after it has dried (but before firing). This paste format can be used to create "hollow-form" items by painting the material directly onto the surface of a burnable core. It can be applied to natural leaves, paper forms (e.g. origami) or many other organic materials to create a perfect, fine silver impression of the original item.

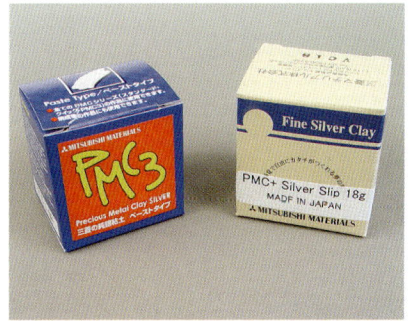

Paste clay type

Paper Sheet:

PMC+ type is formed into ultra-thin, rectangular sheets, either 6 cm (2-3/8") square or 3 cm x 12 cm (1-1/8" x 4-3/4"). This material format contains no water and that means it does not dry out or crack. It feels like a piece of vinyl and is well suited for origami constructions or for simulating fabric or other silver sheet-metal applications. Use decorative craft punches or patterned scissors to punch and shape this material or create a basket weave pattern from several strips. The only limitation is that this material is too thin to be used by itself in a single layer and is most often used laminated or in combination with other clay types as a decorative touch.

Paper sheet type

Safety First - How to Keep it Fun

Precious Metal Clay has been certified to be safe and non-toxic. It conforms to ASTMD D4236 requirements, as indicated on the package insert. However, you still must follow a few simple rules to ensure a safe and enjoyable experience.

- Practice sensible hand washing protocol before starting to work, while in the workshop and especially when you have finished working.
- Do not eat while you are working.
- Pay attention to what you are doing. Remember better safe than sorry!
- Handle sharp items, sharp tools and hot materials carefully.
- The materials and procedures in this book are not intended for children. If you allow children in your work area, it is imperative to keep a close watch on them.
- If you are pregnant or if you or anyone in your family has allergies, you are strongly advised to consult your doctor before engaging in any activity referenced in this book.
- Kilns are hot during and after firing. You cannot be too cautious around a hot kiln. Always use heat-proof gloves and/or long tongs when placing and removing pieces from the kiln while hot.

Helen and Dick Tikal, "Porcelain Doll Earrings" PMC Sheet clay and cubic zirconia gemstone on porcelain, Photo: Ken Devos

Bringing It All Together

*Mary Ann Devos, "Midnight Dancer"
Silver mask pin, bracelet rings, buttons
and leaves mounted on a fabric art doll.
Photo: Ken Devos*

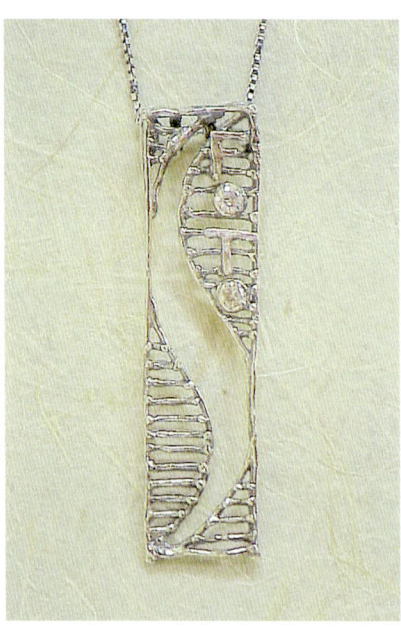

*Sherry Fotopoulos, "Foto Graphic"
Photo: Rob Stegmann*

Safety First - Continued

- Watch the dog, cat, birds or any companion animals you may have and keep them away from the work area. Did you know that you can kill your bird with fumes from burning polymer clay, Styrofoam or over-heated non-stick cookware?
- Use a heat-proof surface in front of the kiln and whenever using a torch. Keep a fire extinguisher handy at all times.
- Do not inhale dust from the kiln fiber blanket, kiln shelves or fumes from any chemicals used in the studio. Use a respirator when necessary.
- Wear eye protection when using power tools such as a Dremel drill, a flex shaft, a butane torch, etc. Read and follow all manufacturers' safety guidelines for tools, chemicals and other materials.

Tools, Equipment & Kilns

Every craft or art activity requires a collection of tools and equipment. Working with metal clay also has some essential tools but the good news is a great many of them are items that you may already have around your home or studio. The most expensive and specialized piece of equipment is the kiln. However, there are some firing alternatives that will allow you to create smaller items without a fancy kiln. Tools and equipment were covered extensively in our first book *Introduction to Precious Metal Clay*. Be sure to consult that book for more detailed information.

Work Table and Surface

PMC is a very clean medium and you will not need a large working space. Many people get started at their kitchen table, a desk in the spare room or a collapsible banquet table in the basement or utility room.

You will also want a smooth portable working surface that sits on your table. This surface will make it easier to salvage unused bits and pieces of the metal clay. Suitable surfaces include: a glass or ceramic kitchen-counter protector, a sheet of standard window glass (with the sharp edges rounded), a sheet of Plexiglas, a smooth plastic placemat, a "self-healing" craft cutting mat, a non-stick flexible baking sheet. Do not use an aluminum surface as this may contaminate the PMC and cause dark spots to appear after firing.

Basic Tools of the Trade

Most metal clay artists have a favorite selection of tools that are kept in a special toolbox off limits to anyone not authorized to use the contents. You would be surprised at the unusual items that turn up in an artists studio disguised as a tool and even more surprised to find out how cleverly they function. Here is a list of items that are essential components in my toolbox.

Basic tools of the trade, clockwise from top left corner: Artist's paintbrushes in assorted sizes, wooden dowel, clay carving tools, craft knife, clay shape cutters, canapé or cookie cutters, thickness slats, PVC roller, playing cards, plastic ruler, dental tools, potter's clay-shaping tools, textured brass plates, lace, rubber stamps, buttons, etc (used for texturing), drinking and stirring straws.

The smooth working surface in the background is a kitchen counter protector made from tempered glass.

Basic Tools of the Trade - List

- Artist's paint brushes in assorted sizes
- Wooden dowels in assorted diameters
- Craft knife, X-Acto® knife, assorted kitchen knifes
- Thickness slats and playing cards
- Plastic ruler (with inch & metric numbers)
- Medical tools (forceps, dental picks, scissors, etc.)
- Polymer shape stampers, cookie cutters
- Organic material for texture and/or burnout
- Drinking and stirring straws, assorted diameters
- Plastic food wrap, small zip-lock baggies
- White craft glue &/or glue stick
- Hand balm or cooking oil - used to coat molds, shapers, fingers and surfaces to prevent the clay from sticking
- Cellophane adhesive tape
- Ring mandrel, wooden and ring sizer
- Tweezers -stainless steel
- Removable adhesive note pads (e.g. Post-it™)
- Standard and decorative-edged scissors
- Patterned paper punches (hearts, stars, etc.)

Shaping Tools

The photo below is selection of shaping tools that I feel are essential for metal clay work, starting at the top left corner they are;

- PVC roller
- Plastic coiling plate
- Double end ball stylus
- Artist's palette knife
- Double ended cutter
- Single ended cutter
- Rubber tipped finishing tools

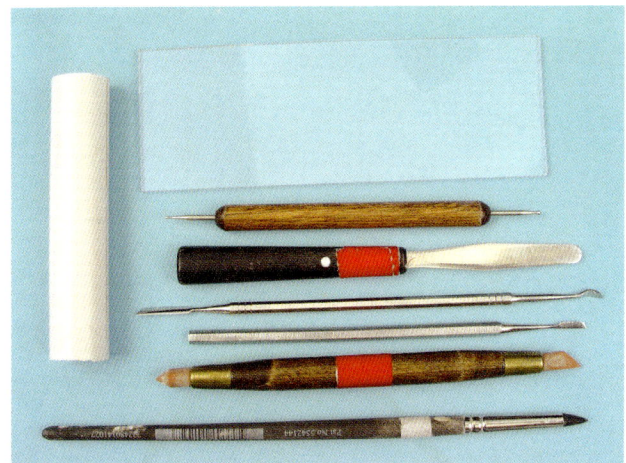

A selection of shaping tools; see list above photo for descriptions.

Bringing It All Together

Texturing materials

Rubber Stamps - watch for copyright use limitations

Rubber stamps are a wonderful source of design and texture for your PMC pieces. If you choose to make use of this resource you must take notice of the copyright restrictions which some stamp manufacturers place on the use of their stamps. Some manufacturers do not allow any commercial use whatsoever. Thankfully many others allow you to use their designs in the creation of any artwork, for both private and commercial purposes. Be sure to find and read the copyright fine print that applies to the stamps you choose to purchase.

Texture Materials

You can use just about anything that has an interesting surface pattern to texture your metal clay art piece. We have used materials from brass buttons to fabric lace and everything in between. In addition hobby/craft stores sell a great variety of materials that you could use. Look in the miniature dollhouse department, the polymer clay section, the rubber stamp collections or the hand-made paper area.

- Rubber texture mat
- Textured brass plate
- Steel punches for leather working
- Lace fabric or any heavily textured material
- Silicone mold (see mold making compounds below)
- Rubber Stamps -commercial or homemade (see notice below left)

Mold Making Compounds

One of the greatest features of PMC is its ability to take on almost any shape or texture. You may want to create a permanent mold to repeat a shape - e.g. a pair of earrings or to repeat a special texture - e.g. flower petals. Almost any mold making material will work such as polymer clay, thermosetting plastics and even silicone based caulking. Or use a special 2-part compound known as Room Temperature Vulcanization (or RTV) that is made especially for this purpose. It's available at most craft stores and it's simple to use. Just follow the product package directions. It will be easier to remove the clay shape if you apply a light coat of cooking oil (or hand balm) to the inside of any mold before pressing the PMC into the mold.

Assembly Tools

You will not need everything in this list right away. However, as you progress in this art form and expand your creative skills you will find more and more of these tools indispensable.

- Jeweler's ball-peen hammer
- Plastic or rawhide mallet
- Jeweler's glue - to secure pinbacks to glass cabochons
- Bezel roller/setter
- Wooden and metal ring mandrels
- Prong pusher - used to bend prongs for stone setting
- Pin vise – for hand drilling
- Magnifying visor-goggles, jeweler's loupe
- Assorted jewelers pliers e.g.: chain, round nose, flat nose, needle nose, side cutter and nylon jaw

Embellishments, Stones and Findings,

Nothing enhances a jewelry piece like a gemstone. No matter if it's lab-grown or natural, the effect is stunning. Then after you've made a beautiful pendant, you will need a necklace chain or cord to hang it from. Earrings require loops or posts, brooches need pin-backs and the list goes on. This list will help you with your shopping.

- Fine silver (.999) wire - 16, 18, 20 and 28 gauge
- Findings: prong-settings for stones, pin-backs, bails, earring hoops, earring 'French' loops, jump rings, split rings, hook clasps, etc.
- Casting grains and beads available in fine silver, brass, bronze, 24k gold
- Lab-grown gemstones: corundum and cubic zirconia (called CZ's)
- Natural stones, precious and semi-precious gems
- Necklace chain in sterling, fine silver, 14K to 24k gold, leather, fabric, etc.

A selection of lab-grown gemstones in an array of colors, plus necklace chains, stone settings, casting grains and natural stones.

Refining and Finishing Tools

It is important to put the finishing touch to your creations after they are bone dry and before putting them in the kiln for final firing. We use an assortment of tools from disposable fingernail files to professional jeweler's files for this process. In addition we have carpenter's sanding blocks, emery cloth, buffer blocks (with a different grit on each surface) and many other surface abrasion tools. A hand-held rotary tool (e.g. Dremel tool) offers tremendous versatility for grinding, drilling and final polishing with an extensive variety of available attachments.

Buffing block, sandpaper and files

Firing - Kilns and Equipment

Programmable Kilns

Firing your piece to fuse the silver or gold particles together (known as sintering) is a very important step in the process of PMC jewelry making. Under-fire your piece and it will be brittle and easily damaged; over-fire it and it will lose the delicate textures and shapes that you spent time working on or worse turn into a melted lump of silver. The good news is we now have programmable kilns available that were developed especially for metal clay and they make this step very easy.

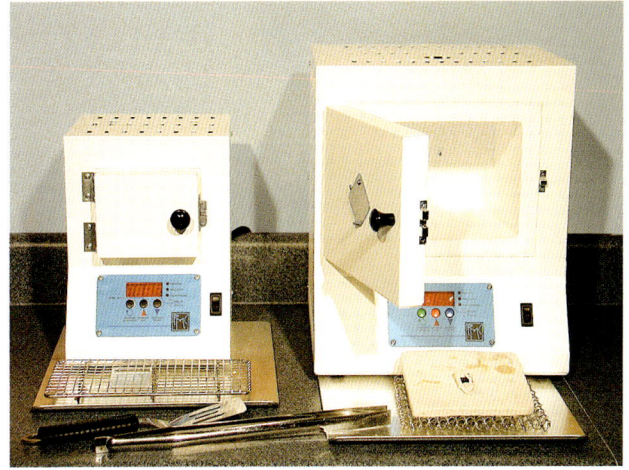

Programmable kilns designed for metal clay firing. The model on the left is an Evenheat 91F with chamber dimensions of 4.5" x 4.5" x 4.5" (11.4 x 11.4 x 11.4 cm). The kiln on right is an Evenheat 360F with chamber dimensions of 8" x 8" x 6" (20.3 x 20.3 x 15.2 cm).

Bringing It All Together

Kiln Firing (continued)

Each clay type has different firing requirements. In addition if your piece has inclusions, that is it 'includes' something other than the metal clay, like fused glass, gemstones, enamels, sterling silver findings, etc. the firing schedule will have to be modified to compensate for the heat requirement of the inclusion. A programmable kiln allows you to make these adjustments with the push of a button. See firing chart with inclusions on page 21.

Butane torch

This hand held torch makes quick work of firing small items. Use it to fire small pendants, charms, clasps, etc. For best results torch fire items made from PMC+ or PMC3, that do not have inclusions other than CZ's or lab grown gemstones and are no thicker than 1/4" (6 mm) and no larger than 1-1/2" (38 mm).

This small hand held Butane torch can generate enough heat to fire small PMC3 and PMC+ pieces, such as rings or pendants, in only a few minutes. The torch has a child resistant design and meets all CPSC safety regulations.

Firing Accessories

- Heatproof surface, to protect under and in front of the kiln (insulated cookie sheets work well for this)
- Long tongs (outdoor BBQ type) for removing and replacing hot kiln shelves
- Digital minute timer
- Tweezers, long handled to help position items on a hot kiln shelf
- Drying / cooling rack: a baker's wire rack with small mesh screen
- Ceramic fiber kiln shelf
- Ceramic fiber blanket
- Hi-temp protective gloves/mitts

Mary Ellin D'Agostino, "Octopus Pin"
Photo: Mary Ellin D'Agostino

Burnishing and Polishing Tools

After firing a PMC piece, the surface will have a matte white appearance instead of the shiny silver that you might expect. The white color is due to an irregular and slightly rough surface. A stainless steel wire brush will quickly give the item a brushed matte finish. Then use one of the burnishing tools to compress and smooth the surface areas that you want to have a bright shiny finish.

- Agate burnisher - wide
- Agate burnisher - narrow
- Steel burnisher - straight
- Steel jeweler's burnisher - curved

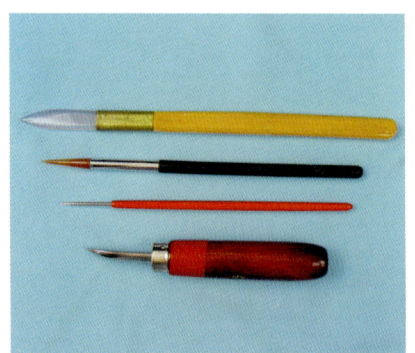

A selection of hand-burnishing tools, from top; wide agate burnisher, narrow agate burnisher, straight steel burnisher (PMC model shown), curved steel burnisher.

If you're looking for an overall shiny surface use a rotary tumbler-polisher with mixed stainless steel shot. These machines are available from jewelry suppliers and will make quick work for a bright mirror finish (see page 23).

Fundamental Techniques

Moisture Retention and Storage:

Open a new package of PMC lump clay and you will encounter a soft, smooth, luscious clay that is a joy to work with. At once it begins to lose moisture and depending on the humidity level in your studio, it could be too dry to sculpt within minutes. So open the package, break off enough for your project and immediately return the unused portion to the original foil package, then squeeze the air from the package and zip-seal it. If you are going to leave the clay stored for a while you may want to add a few drops of water to keep the clay in top condition.

As you work with the clay it will dry out. Use a moist paintbrush to apply a little bit of clean water to the surface of the clay. Allow a few seconds for the water to sink into the clay before continuing. You will soon get a feel for the clay and will sense that it is drying out. Visualize how supple it felt right out of the package and try to maintain that same consistency as you work it.

Linda Bernstein, "Goddess Necklace"
Photo: Rob Stegmann

Forming, Shaping and Texturing

Tools for working with the clay are straightforward and uncomplicated. Our standard toolbox includes: artists' paint brushes, potter's clay shapers, cutters and texture tools and other assorted everyday items found around the home or shop. See pages 10-12 for tools and equipment.

There are really only 4 basic forming techniques that you need to master. They are; slab rolling, coil forming, syringe extrusion and paste coating. Most other fabrication steps are a variation or combination of these basic procedures.

Slab Rolling

Start by lightly coating your work surface, your hands and the PVC roller with cooking oil or hand balm to prevent sticking. Pinch off a piece of lump clay and roll it into a tight ball between your palms. Place this ball on the work surface and flatten it slightly with your hand. Now place two stacks of playing cards, one on either side of the clay to function as a thickness guide and use a PVC roller to flatten the clay. A 2-3 card stack will yield a thin slab of approximately 1/32" (.8 mm); 4-5 cards will produce a medium thickness 3/64" (1.5 mm); and 6 cards give a thick slab of about 5/64" (2 mm). Remember, PMC+ and PMC3 clay are going to shrink by 12% and PMC Standard will shrink by almost 1/3 so be sure to allow for this shrinkage in your design.

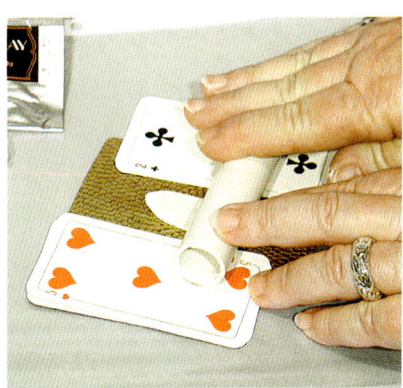

Slab rolling using playing cards as spacers. This 3 card stack will make a medium thick slab of approximately 1/32" (.8 mm). Notice the use of a brass plate under the clay to give the surface a soft texture.

Bringing It All Together

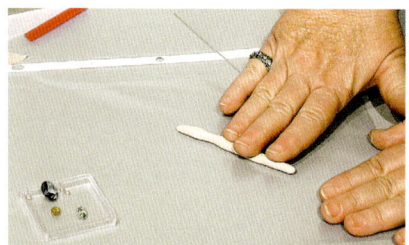
Roll the coil first by hand

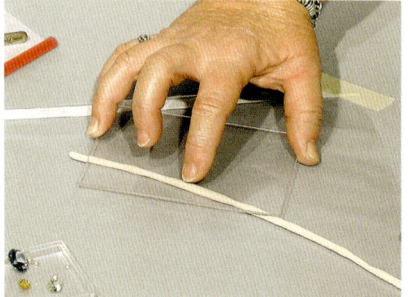
Finish the coil with a 'roll-plate'

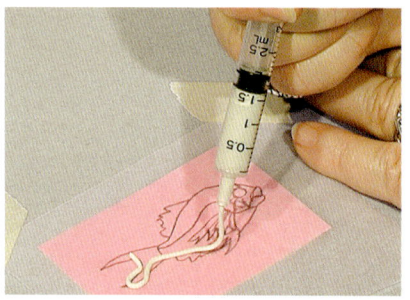
Syringe extrusion without the fine tip

Syringe with the tip on for a finer line

Using a brush to reposition the extrusions

Coil 'Snake' Forming

Start by lightly coating your work surface, your hands and the Plexiglas roll-plate with cooking oil or hand balm to prevent sticking. Pinch off a piece of lump clay from the package and roll it between your palms to create a thick 'coil' roll. Place this thick coil on the work surface and continue to work the coil with your fingers keeping it even along its length. Finish the coil using a Plexiglas roll-plate to create a uniform diameter. Continue to work the coil until it is reduced to the diameter that you need for your design. Be sure to keep the coil hydrated by brushing on a little water and allowing the water to soak in. This will keep the clay pliable and prevent it from cracking.

Syringe Extrusion

Syringe extrusion decoration is one of the truly magical applications available only to metal clay artists. One of my favorite techniques is to create a simple filigree design on paper and trace the lines with the clay extrusion. Use syringe extrusions to form gemstone settings, surface textures, patterns and even to create entire pieces.

You can extrude a design directly on your work surface, as I have done in this fish filigree design, or extrude directly onto another clay shape. Push about 1/4" (6 mm) of extrusion from the syringe and touch the point end of the clay extrusion onto the surface to "lock" the clay string down. Apply firm and steady pressure to the plunger to extrude the clay string, slowly lifting the syringe from the paper until you are holding it about 1/2" to 1" (1 to 2.5 cm) above the surface. Try to maintain one continuous line of clay, laying it down as if it were wet string. You will find it easier to control the line if you place your free hand under the syringe hand to act as a support. When you have finished extruding your design stop pushing on the syringe plunger and twist slightly to break off the clay string. If the extrusion is not position exactly as you wanted it, simply use a fine point brush damped with a little water to adjust it. This extrusion technique will take some practice, but once you have mastered it an entire world of creative possibilities will materialize.

Paste Coating

One of the most popular projects for new PMC artists is to coat the underside of a leaf with the paste clay. When the piece is fired the leaf burns away to reveal an intricately textured replica of the leaf in pure silver. The opportunity to transfer pure silver to an art piece using a simple paint stroke is an amazing ability that is unique to the metal clay experience. But paste clay is so much more than that; it is the glue that holds everything together – literally. A dab of paste clay is used to join two separate components during fabrication and it is used to smooth edges and fill spaces. Paste clay is used to add wet textures, like ripples, wrinkles or waves. Then after an item has dried, the paste is used to refine the shape and to fill cracks and fissures, before it is sent for final kiln firing.

When working with PMC+ or PMC3 use the paste clay made specifically for that product type, although PMC3 will work well with either type. PMC Standard is not available in paste form but it is easy to make your own by mixing a small amount of water with a little clay.

Shaping and Texturing

When the metal clay is still wet it can be textured with just about anything that has a texture. We have used antique buttons, seashells, fabric, handmade paper, tree bark, dried pasta, plastic toys, screen, coins... you get the idea. If it has a texture chances are it will leave an impression on the clay. Just remember to put a light coating of cooking oil or hand balm on the item before pressing it into the wet clay to prevent it from sticking and have fun. Of course there are hundreds of texturing devices available commercially from art & craft supply shops, look in the various departments for polymer clay, dollhouses, leather craft, model trains and of course the rubber stamp selections (see page 12). Plus you can add freehand textures using clay shaping tools, sharpened sticks and numerous other instruments that can be adapted for this purpose.

Once the clay has stiffened to leather-hard or fully dried to the bone-dry state you can continue to texture, shape and refine it with chisels, files, scrapers, emery paper, etc. Linoleum carving tools, available from art supply stores, are ideal for carving bone-dry clay. These tools are available in several tip shapes and sizes that will allow you to create various effects.

Gemstones, Findings and Mountings

Many man-made or 'lab-grown' gemstones can be safely fired in the kiln as part of a silver clay sculpture. If you are not certain that the gemstones you have will fire safely you should test them before you use them in one of your creations. To test a stone simply place it in the kiln while you are doing a standard firing of other pieces to see if it holds its color and shape. It is a good idea to cover the 'test stones' with a piece of ceramic fiber blanket to prevent damage to the inside of the kiln in case they burst.

Gemstones - Cubic Zirconia

Cubic Zirconia gemstones (CZ's for short) are man-made and downright stunning. CZ's are eye-catching, available in a significant range of colors and they look first-class, so use and wear them with pleasure. CZ's are ideal in combination with PMC since they are very heat tolerant (they can even be fired with a torch), they are inexpensive and they look impressive in any jewelry piece. One note of caution: Not all CZ's are created equal. If you are not sure your CZ supplier has heat-tested their stones for color and structural stability you will need to do this testing yourself before using a stone in one of your pieces.

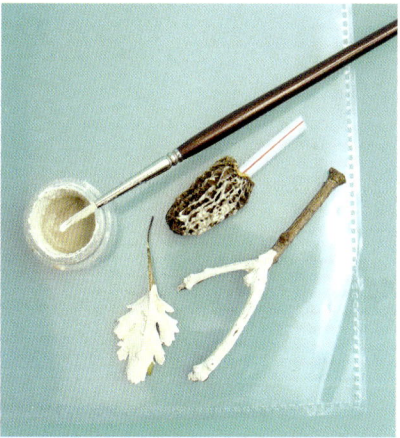

Using paste clay to coat twigs and leaves

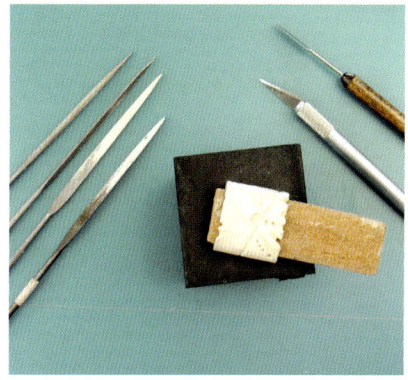

Dry carving a design on a clay ring bead

*Vera Lightstone, "Shaman Mask"
Displayed on a sterling stand,
Photo: Rob Stegmann*

Bringing It All Together 17

Mary Ann Devos, "Green Fields"
Photo: Ken Devos

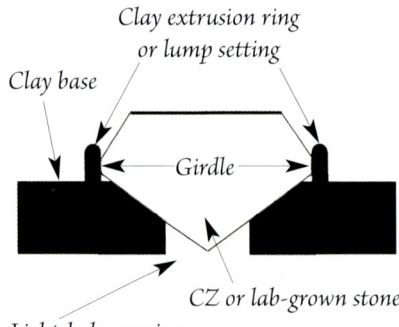

Illustration for stone setting with PMC

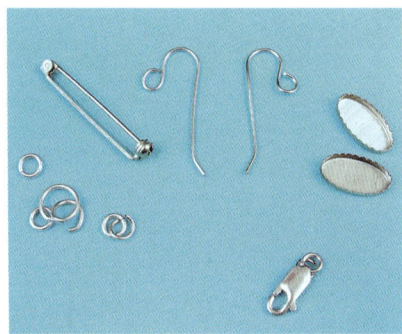

Examples of jewelry findings, clockwise from top left corner, brooch pin back, earring wires, bezel cups (for natural stones), lobster claw clasp and jump rings.

Gemstones - Synthetic

Laboratory grown or synthetic stones have chemical compositions that are identical to the natural stones. The manufacturing process speeds the crystal formation that takes nature hundreds of years. Most of these stones do not have inclusions (impurities) and kiln-firing does not normally fracture them. At the same time, you must be careful not to cause thermal shock by reducing the temperature of the piece too rapidly after firing.

Gemstones - Natural

Some natural gemstones can withstand kiln firing but only stones that are at least a 7 or higher on the MOHS scale (a measure of the relative hardness of minerals). Stones such as granite, quartz and the corundum family meet this benchmark. Other natural stones are too soft to fire successfully e.g. bone, fossils, turquoise and amber. Stones lower than 7 MOHS are at great risk of fracturing and may even crumble in the kiln at temperatures of 1110°F / 600°C to 1650°F / 900°C. Some stones will survive the heat but may undergo a color shift or may have small inclusions that could result in cracks later on. To be completely safe with natural gemstones in your piece use the more traditional bezel or prong stone mounting techniques.

Stone Setting With PMC

PMC lump clay and syringe clay provide two easy ways to set CZ's and other lab grown stones. In either method you must remember to keep the top of the stone level and ensure the clay or syringe captures the girdle of the stone to prevent it from falling out (see illustration at left).

Lump clay method: Use a small ball of clay, about twice the size of the stone, and attach it to your clay piece using paste. Use a plastic straw that is slightly smaller than the diameter of the stone to punch an opening through the ball and the clay underneath creating a light-hole. Use tweezers to place the stone on this light-hole opening and push it into the clay to below its girdle.

Syringe clay method: Use a plastic straw to punch the light hole through the clay then create a collar of syringe clay around the hole tall enough to cover the stone's girdle. Place the stone and push it into the syringe collar.

Findings

'Findings' is a jeweler's term that refers to pre-manufactured components that are added to a jewelry piece. Examples of findings are: earring loops & studs, jump rings, pendant bails, clasps, brooch pins, stone bezels, etc. (gemstones are not usually described as a finding). Findings can be made from pure silver, silver alloy, gold and many other metals. Pure or fine silver is defined as .999 silver and is the same composition as all PMC silver types. Sterling .925 is an alloy combination of silver (92.5%) and copper (7.5%). The addition of copper makes sterling stronger than fine silver and because of this many findings are made of sterling.

Sterling Silver Components and PMC

Unfortunately the copper content in sterling .925 is more reactive to heat. When sterling is subjected to high heat firing (temperatures above 1350°F) it becomes brittle and more likely to fracture. In addition the copper content will oxidize leaving a blackened metal surface referred to as 'fire-scale'. For these reasons we do not recommended firing sterling with PMC Standard or PMC+ clay types. However, sterling components can be successfully combined with PMC3 due to the relatively low firing temperature.

Mountings

If you need to incorporate fine silver findings in PMC Standard or PMC+ items, be sure to use a thicker gauge than findings made from sterling. However, when delicate findings are required for earring studs, prong gemstone mounts (for natural stones), small clasps, etc., you will want to take advantage of the added strength of sterling. These finding parts are easily added during the finishing stage (after firing) by solder them into position using a small butane torch and silver solder. Some fire scale will develop near the solder area but this can be removed by placing your piece in a container of jewelers pickle solution to soak for a few minutes. Then remove and rinse in clear water.

Soldering a sterling silver pin-back into position using a small butane torch.

Drying, Refining and Firing

The Importance of Drying

It is essential that all projects be thoroughly and completely dried before firing. If an item is fired before it is bone-dry any moisture trapped inside will quickly turn to steam and could burst through the surface creating a small crater or an extreme crack. Basically there are 2 methods for drying your sculpture, air-drying or heat-drying.

Air-drying is the most straightforward approach. Simply place your item in a dry location, support any areas that could droop and wait until it is dry. The time it will take to get to the bone-dry stage will depend largely on the humidity of the location. High humidity areas will need more time, possibly up to 24 hours, while low humidity locations will require much less time.

Heat drying is certainly faster and more controllable than air-drying. The most common appliances used for metal clay drying are: a food dehydrator, a small hair dryer, an electric heated serving tray, an electric griddle (fry-pan), a toaster oven or even a standard kitchen oven. You only need a small travel-duty hair dryer that you can use hand-held or make the task easier by building a simple drying-box like the one shown here (at right). An electric heated serving tray should be set on medium to high, electric griddle set to low 150°F/66°C, set toaster oven also to 150°F/66°C and use a standard kitchen oven only as a last resort, set at the lowest warming temperature.

Sondra Busch, "Memory Leaf"
Photo: Rob Stegmann

A simple drying-box using a hair dryer

An electric food dehydrator

Dehydrator

An electric food dehydrator could easily be said to have been made for the job of drying metal clay. These units gently heat, circulate the air and draw humidity away from anything placed inside them. They have open-mesh trays (often several layers) and make quick work of total controlled drying. As a bonus they draw very little power and are very economical to operate.

It is Dry Yet?

No matter which drying technique you utilize you must test to ensure your piece is completely dry. Place your piece on a mirror and hold it there for 5-10 seconds, then pick it up. If you see a "ghost" on the mirror this is actually a water vapor mark indicating the piece is not completely dry.

Refining

This is the final rehearsal before the opening night curtain, a sort of 'dry-run' if you will pardon the pun. While it is possible to shape your piece after firing it is certainly much easier to file or sand bone-dry clay than solid metal. If cracks or other blemishes materialized during the drying process, simply fill these in with the paste (and re-dry). You still have time to add another decorative flourish, a gemstone, a hanging loop or to drill a hole. But most importantly you have an opportunity to smooth and refine your piece with sandpaper (use silicon paper from 300 to 2000 grit), emery board (a.k.a. fingernail files), gouges, chisels and shape files. Here's a secret tip, use an alcohol free wet wipe to make the surfaces ultra smooth. Spending time to finish your piece in this state will improve your final results tremendously.

Firing

Firing will transform your sculpture from a lackluster lump of dried clay into a magnificent piece of sculpted fine silver or 22K gold. Precious Metal Clay is nothing more than extremely small particles of precious metal, either .999 pure silver or 22K gold, suspended in a water based organic binder. During the firing process the binder burns away leaving a fully fused silver or gold piece. Shrinkage occurs as a result of the sintering process as the precious metal particles fuse together, filling in the space that was originally occupied by the binder.

There are several methods and kiln types that can be used to fire PMC successfully. These include butane torch firing, PMC Hot Pot kiln and the programmable kiln made for metal clay work (see description on page 13).

A programmable kiln is the most accurate and reliable firing method. Simply set the firing schedule for the PMC type that you are using, allow for any heat-sensitive material included in your piece (e.g. glass, natural stones, etc.), turn the kiln on and let it do its work.

Be sure to refer to the specific firing instructions for inclusions on next page.

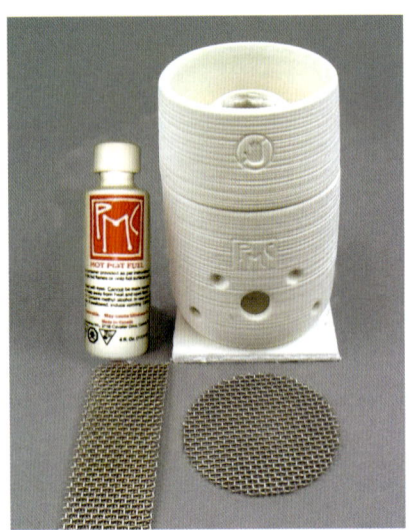

PMC 'Hot Pot' kiln
PMC3 can be easily and economically fired in this ingenious alcohol-fueled kiln. The kiln is strategically shaped to enable the gelled alcohol to bring the kiln interior to the optimum firing temperature for the correct length of time to fire PMC3 clay material. Simply place the ceramic fuel cup, filled to capacity with the gelled fuel, in the bottom of the kiln, place your PMC3 items on the metal screen shelf, put on the lid and light the fuel through the lower hole in the kiln. In approximately 20 minutes the fuel will be burned and your silver clay item will be finished firing.

Product Type	Firing Temperature	Firing Time	Inclusions
PMC Standard	1650°F / 900°C	2 hours	Pre-fired Gold Parts
PMC+	1650°F / 900°C	10 minutes	Burnout Materials
PMC+	1560°F / 850°C	20 minutes	Cubic Zirconia
PMC+	1470°F / 800°C	30 minutes	Synthetic Stones
PMC3	1290°F / 700°C	10 minutes	Some Natural Stones
PMC3	1200°F / 650°C	20 minutes	Sterling Components
PMC3	1110°F / 600°C	45 minutes	Fused Glass
PMC 22K Gold	1650°F / 900°C	10 minutes	Burnout Materials
PMC 22K Gold	1560°F / 850°C	30 minutes	Cubic Zirconia
PMC 22K Gold	1380°F / 750°C	60 minutes	Synthetic Stones
PMC 22K Gold	1290°F / 700°C	90 minutes	Some Natural Stones

This firing chart illustrates time and temperature schedules for the various clay types fired with some typical inclusions.

Note: Any inclusion that can withstand a higher temperature can be safely fired in a lower temperature schedule, but not the other way around.

Firing with Glass Inclusions and PMC3

Firing art glass and metal at the same time requires a modification in the firing schedule. The temperature and hold time are different but more importantly the rate at which the kiln temperature increases from cold to the desired target temperature is also different. Glass is more susceptible to thermal shock and it is important to increase the temperature more slowly than with PMC3 alone.

The temperature ramp speed (increase in temperature) must be at a moderate rate of about 1500°F/ 816°C per hour. In other words it should take about 45 minutes to reach the desired hold temperature of 1110°F / 600°C. Once that temperature has been reached you must hold it there for 45 minutes.

After the 45 minutes of hold time, the item with its glass inclusion can be "crash cooled" by opening the kiln door to allow it to cool rapidly from 1110°F / 600°C to 950°F / 510°C. Open the door and watch the pyrometer as the kiln temperature decreases. When the temperature reaches about 850°F / 455°C close the kiln door. Retained heat in the kiln chamber and walls will cause the temperature to go back up after a few minutes. If the temperature goes above 1000°F / 535°C, repeat the "crash cool" process until the temperature remains below the 1000°F / 535°C point. This crash cooling process will prevent devitrification (hazing or clouding) of the glass surface. Finally, close the kiln door and leave it closed (do not even think about taking a peek) until the kiln has cooled slowly to room temperature (this will take several hours; it's best to simply leave it overnight).

CeCe Wire, "Asian Assemblage," Pendant with Chinese coin, 2001

Bringing It All Together

The white color is due to a slightly irregular surface that does not reflect light very well. This results in surface that has a dull, matte white appearance.

Hattie Sanderson, "Galaxy Pendant"
Photo: Hattie Sanderson

Mary Ann Devos, "Hand-made Clasps"
Photo: Rob Stegmann

Finishing, Polishing and Antiquing

You can hardly contain yourself long enough to allow the kiln to cool before getting a glimpse at the shiny silver piece that you've created. You open the door and ... don't panic! The matte white exterior is perfectly normal. It's the way all fine silver looks after kiln firing. The white color is due to a slightly irregular surface that does not reflect light very well and that results in a dull, not-shiny appearance. That is why this next step is perhaps the most gratifying of them all, when you take your piece to the next level of expert presentation. You might want to give your piece a bright mirror finish or a brushed satin look or perhaps some combination of the two. Depending on your artistic whim you may choose to impart a patina ranging from a light bronze to an antique black.

Brushed Satin Matte Finish

A good brushing with a stainless steel or brass wire brush will result in a pleasing matte finish. As you brush you will begin to see a dull shine, beyond a certain point no amount of extra brushing will produce a brighter shine. A brass bristled brush produces a somewhat brighter finish as compared to the matte finish of stainless steel bristles. Brushing with a dry brush is effective on simple pieces however many artist's feel they get better results brushing with a mild solution of liquid soap and water or baking soda and water. In addition to the differences produced by a brass vs. stainless steel brush you can create distinctive effects by brushing in a single direction only or try alternating the strokes at 45° or 90° to one another to produce a cross-hatch pattern. Experiment with various brushing patterns to discover the many unique effects that are possible.

Gleaming Polished Shine

There is little doubt that a bright shiny silver object is attention grabbing. We use phrases in our everyday language like 'shines like silver' and 'slick as silver' to describe the glistening finish on non-silver items. Your precious metal clay piece can take on a professional mirror finish with only a little extra effort.

We know that the white coloration of a just-fired item is the result of an uneven surface. Therefore to achieve a high shine finish we need to smooth that uneven surface, in effect we need to push the high points down and fill in the low areas. Start with an even wire-brushed finish (unless there are areas on the piece that you want to leave in the raw-fired state). The 3 common ways to achieve a polished finish are: by hand burnishing using an agate or steel burnisher tool, by tumbling with stainless steel shot in a jewelry tumbler and by using polishing papers and/or sponge sanding pads.

Hand Burnishing

Hand burnishing provides the artist an opportunity to selectively polish some areas while leaving other areas in the matte-brushed or raw-fired state. Bunishers are particularly effective at polishing the raised areas in a textured piece. Start from a brushed matte finish using the stainless steel brush. Place your item on a rubber block and press the burnishing tool firmly against the silver surface. Rub the tool back and forth across the silver, taking care not to scratch the surface with the point of the tool. It should not take long to bring up a beautiful shine, especially if you were careful to sand and finish your piece completely in the bone-dry clay state before firing.

Hand burnishing on a rubber block

Jeweler's Rotary Tumbler

For an overall bright finish you can't beat the ease of an electric rotary tumbler with stainless steel mixed shot. Start from a brushed matte finish using the stainless steel brush, then place your piece or several pieces at the same time, in the tumbler. Add just enough burnishing fluid (or 1 drop of dish soap along with water) to cover the jewelry and the stainless steel shot. Turn it on and let it tumble away. Depending on the effect that you desire your piece may be done in 20 to 30 minutes but some items can take from 1 to 2 hours. It is a good idea to check your pieces periodically until they have the appearance you're looking for. Another advantage to tumbling with stainless steel shot is it will work-harden your piece by compacting the silver and making it stronger.

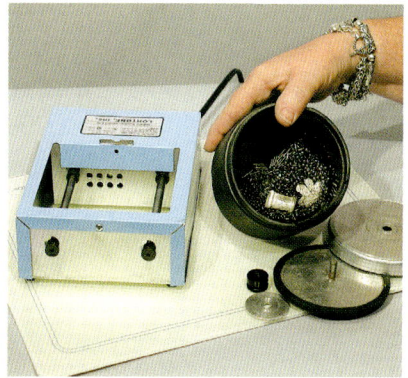
You can't beat the ease of an electric rotary tumbler with stainless steel shot

Professional 'Mirror Quality' Shine

A rotary tumbler with stainless steel mixed shot over 1 to 2 hours will give your item a beautiful shine. However if you are looking for the ultimate professional mirror shine you will have to employ a mixture of patience and elbow grease. A super bright mirror finish requires final polishing using progressively finer abrasives and polishing materials. This technique works best on smooth surfaces. Use fine emery cloth or sponge sanding pads and polishing papers (made by 3M) that start at medium grit (comparable to 600 to 800 grit) then move through finer and super fine grades (comparable to 1000 to 2000 grit). Start with a medium grade abrasive material and be sure to keep the grit wet as you rub your piece in small circles. Rinse and clean your piece and the sandpaper often. Polish the entire surface of your piece using progressively finer material until you have reached a high shine. The final professional touch is to use a quality silver polish and buff your piece until you have produced a sparkle and shine that will require sunglasses for someone to look directly at it.

Artisans of Oblique, "Ephemera"
Photo: Ken Devos

Bringing It All Together

Marlynda Taylor, "Forrest Collage"
Photo: Ken Devos

Soak and swirl in the warm liver of sulfur solution for a few seconds then remove

Removing the patina from some areas to highlight the silver for contrast

Antique Patina

The elegant and mysterious quality of an antique patina has the ability to shift some silver sculptures from ordinary to extraordinary. The antiquing process is so easy to do. Simply dip your piece into a liver of sulfur solution and watch as the surface instantly takes on an aged and refined appearance.

The liver of sulfur patina process produces colors in an ordered progression from yellow-gold, to rosy-amber, red-mauve, bluish-purple, purple-black and finally full black. The colors produced by a patina are not entirely stable and will change over time due to tarnishing that is customary to all silver. If you wish to protect the color from tarnish, seal the surface with jeweler's lacquer.

The Process

Liver of sulfur releases an odor that is quite pungent (often compared to the smell of rotten eggs) so work in a well ventilated area. Dissolve a pea size chunk of liver of sulfur in 1/2 cup (120 ml) of hot (almost boiling) water. The temperature of the solution and the dip/soak time will determine the subsequent color. Use an insulated mug or a portable hotplate to help retain the heat (do not let the solution get above 150°F / 65°C). A coffee mug warmer works nicely for this. The solution will be most effective for only a few hours so mix just enough for one session.

Make sure your item is clean (does not have finger smudges or hand balm on it), grasp it with stainless steel tweezers and dip it into the warm solution. Soak and swirl it for a few seconds then remove and rinse it in a bowl of clean water. If you want the color darker, dip and rinse again. Repeat this dipping and rinsing process allowing the color change to progress through the color range. As soon as you have attained the color you want, soak the item in clean water for several minutes to stop the patina development.

A variety of effects can be achieved by altering the finishing process prior to dipping. Leave some portions of the white-colored surface unpolished or wire brush some areas and burnish others. Try dipping the piece at different angles and/or hold it only partially submerged in the solution to get a variegated, multi-color effect.

After the patina has been applied, the piece can be further enhanced by selectively removing the patina from some areas to highlight the silver for contrast. Use a jeweler's rouge polishing cloth or extra fine grit emery paper (wet or dry) to expose the silver on the raised areas while leaving the antique patina in the recessed areas.

There are other antiquing solutions available from jewelry suppliers that can be used in place of the liver of sulfur. These alternate solutions produce different antiquing effects depending on their chemical make-up. Always follow the manufacturer's instructions for satisfactory results.

Seed Beads - Front

Marlynda Taylor,
"Seed Beads Pendant"
Photo: Rob Stegmann

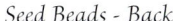

Seed Beads - Back

Mary Ann Devos, "Tribal Necklace" Photo: Ken Devos

PMC and Bead Garden

It can take hours of effort to create a spectacular bead project. It only makes sense to embellish your beadwork with hand-made, solid silver PMC clasps and accent pieces.

Mary Ann Devos, "Flower Power Necklace" Photo: Ken Devos

Mary Ann Devos, "Sun Worship Necklace" Photo: Rob Stegmann

Bringing It All Together

25

Add the excitement of glass to your sculptural PMC3 projects. Use glass as a color embellishment to augment the overall design.

Mary Ann Devos, "A Peas Me"
Photo: Ken Devos

Hattie Sanderson, "Feline Fantasy"
Photo: Hattie Sanderson

Chapter 1
PMC & Glass

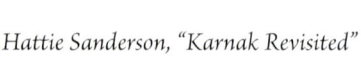

Mary Ann Devos, "Meditation"
Photo: Ken Devos

Hattie Sanderson, "Karnak Revisited"
Photo: Hattie Sanderson

Mary Ann Devos, "Atlas Tierra"
Photo: Rob Stegmann

"Tequila Sunrise"

"Back in Black"

Spontaneous PMC3 syringe work captures and intensifies the brilliance of dichroic glass cabochons.

Chapter 1
PMC & Glass

"Third Trimester"

"Dilly Diva"

"Zoom, Zoom"

All items on this page were created by: Mary Ann Devos (glass cabochon in Dilly Diva was made by Elisa Cossey) All photos: Ken Devos

"Captured Glass Bead"

Precious Metal Clay and Glass

27

Garnish Dish

Floating Silver Designs In Glass
By Mary Ann Devos

These garnish dishes are fused glass with PMC+ sheet inclusions. They are fun and easy to make in a small kiln.

Materials & Equipment

PMC+ sheet type clay

Fusing glass 1 piece clear and 1 piece colored, cut to size and shape required for plate mold

Glass stringers and/or Glass frit (for decoration)

Note: All glass must have the same 'tested compatible' COE number

Kaiser-Lee™ fiberboard (to make slump mold) or ceramic slump mold suitable for small plate

Thinfire separator paper

Decorative paper punches

Decorative scissors

Carving tools

Soap and water (for glass cleaning)

Programmable kiln

Fiberboard kiln shelf

Mary Ann Devos, "Dragonfly Dish," Photo: Ken Devos

Procedure:

1. Create a number of decorative cutouts from single thickness PMC+ sheet. There are literally hundreds of patterned paper punches available featuring designs ranging from stars to zodiac symbols or from flowers to dragonflies (as you see in the dish above). Make your choice and punch away. Or you could create your own custom cutout designs using decorative-edge scissors or a craft knife.

2. Fire the PMC+ sheet cutout designs in your kiln at 1650°F / 900°C for 10 minutes.

3. Brush them with a stainless steel wire brush then place them in the rotary tumbler for about 20 minutes to polish to a high shine.

3. Lay a piece of Thinfire™ separator paper on your kiln shelf then arrange the fired and polished silver pieces in a pleasing pattern on the firing paper. Carefully clean both sides of the clear glass piece and place it on top of the silver pieces. Make sure no part of the glass extends beyond the Thinfire™ paper.

4. Place the shelf in the kiln and fire it to 1450°F / 788°C using a ramp speed of 2000°F / 1090°C per hour (this means it should take about 45 minutes to reach 1450°F / 788°C) Soak the glass at 1450°F / 788°C for 10 minutes, turn off the kiln, open the door and crash cool to 950°F / 537°C. Close the door and let the kiln cool until it reaches room temperature.

5. Next we need to create the cavity mold using a piece of Kaiser-Lee™ fiberboard. Start with a piece of fiberboard that is slightly larger than the glass blanks. Draw a square, an oval, a circle or any shape you choose. This shape will form the bowl portion of the dish. Follow the line using a craft knife and cut only partway through the fiberboard. Use a putty knife to carve and gouge out the cavity making sure the bottom is level and a consistent depth. Use you finger to smooth the edges of the mold cavity cutout to round it off slightly.

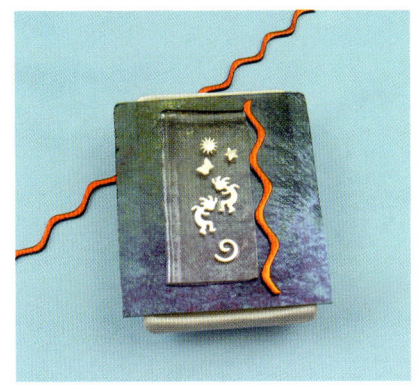

6. Place a piece of Thinfire™ separator paper to cover the top of the mold. The separator paper will prevent the glass from sticking and will drop into the cavity along with the glass during slumping.

7. Carefully clean both sides of the colored glass piece and place it on the mold, centered over the slump hole. Clean and place the clear glass with silver inclusions on the colored glass making sure the silver inclusions are between the clear and colored layer.

8. Place the kiln shelf and mold assembly into the kiln, check to ensure the assembly is still properly aligned then close the kiln door.

9. Program the kiln to a very slow ramp up rate of 750°F / 400°C per hour to 1500°F / 815°C. Hold for 10 minutes. Open the door to check that the dish has fully slumped into the dropout hole. If it has not fully slumped, close the door and soak for another 10 minutes and check it again. When the slump is finished keep the door open to crash cool to 950°F / 537°C.

10. Hold that temperature for 30 minutes to properly anneal the glass. Resist the temptation to open the kiln door! Just turn the kiln off and allow it to cool until it is at room temperature.

Take the dish from the kiln and clean it in a container of water to remove the Thinfire™ residue.

Observations & Alternatives

This process can be accomplished in one firing by placing both layers of glass on the mold with the polished PMC silver between the layers. However, the single fire method has a tendency to trap air bubbles around the silver inserts that may detract from the overall effect of the inclusions.

For more information on the art of glass fusing we recommend a book by Petra Kaiser 'Introduction to Glass Fusing' ISBN: 919985-38-6 published by Wardell Publications Inc.

Dichroic Glass And Fine Silver Brooch

Using PMC3 Syringe In A New Technique With Glass
By Mary Ann Devos

The straightforward techniques of creating with PMC enable glass fusing artists to add silver adornments to their projects while opening up a world of shimmering color to silver jewelry artists. The lower temperature firing schedule makes PMC3 ideally suited to combine with glass. The glass can be fired along with the silver clay without having to expose the glass to full-fuse temperatures.

Materials & Equipment

PMC3 syringe
Dichroic glass cabochon 1" to 1-1/2" (25 to 38 mm) in diameter we used COE 90 glass from Coatings By Sandberg

Small artist's brush
Freezer or Teflon paper
Hair dryer
Stainless steel wire brush
Burnishing tool
Pin back
Soap and water
  (for glass cleaning)
E-6000™ adhesive
Programmable kiln
Fiberboard kiln shelf

Mary Ann Devos, "Dichro Diva"
Photo: Rob Stegmann

Procedure:

1. For this colorful pin I choose an interesting dichroic glass cabochon that is actually two cabochons that were tack fused together when they were originally made. Start by placing your cabochon on a Teflon™ baking sheet or a piece of freezer paper.

2. Since the cabochon I am using is relatively heavy I need to make sure the silver bezel is strong enough to support it. I will use the PMC3 syringe without a tip and encircle the perimeter of the cabochon 2 or 3 times to create a multiple layer of extrusions (for this project I used a modified figure 8 pattern).

3. When you have finished laying down the syringe lines adjust them as necessary using a dampened artist's brush.

4. Now add more syringe clay to accentuate your design. I used a combination of loops and spirals. The idea is to 'shrink lock' the clay to the glass to hold it securely. I try to place the extrusions close to the glass edges, avoiding gaps, to ensure the clay fully encompasses the cabochon. PMC3 shrinks about 12% as it sinters (fuses together) and this will impart an even closer fit around the glass.

5. Evaluate your design and if you choose, add some CZ's, casting grains, pure silver wire flourishes or other embellishments.

6. When you have finished fabrication, dry your piece completely. See pages 19-20 for drying techniques and how to test for dryness.

7. It is much easier to improve and perfect the clay in the bone-dry state rather than after it has been fired into solid metal. When refining is complete, clean any clay particles and dust from the surface of the glass and make sure you have not left any fingerprints behind.

8. Fire the piece in a programmable kiln using the slow-fire schedule with a hold temperature of 1110°F / 600°C and the hold time at 45-60 minutes. The slow-fire schedule will set a ramp-up speed (increase in temperature) of 1500°F/ 816°C per hour. In other words it will take about 45 minutes to reach the hold temperature of 1110°F / 600°C.

9. After firing allow it to cool slowly to room temperature. See page 21 for more details on firing with glass inclusions.

10. When the piece is cool remove it from the kiln and finish the silver. Start by brushing the silver with the stainless steel wire brush to give it a matte finish. Then use a hand burnisher to bring the entire surface or portions of the silver to a bright shine.

11. Attach a sterling pin back using E-6000 or similar adhesive for bonding glass to metal.

Mary Ann Devos, "To The Point"
Photo: Ken Devos

Observations & Alternatives

The lower firing temperatures for PMC3 (vs. other PMC silver types) allow the artist to create a delicate frame around a glass cabochon. The reduced weight as compared to hand-rolled clay coils makes the pieces more comfortable to wear.

You can build a fine silver wire framework into the piece to permit the addition of chains or charms. Start by forming a silver wire structure then wrap it around the cabochon shape. Proceed by adding the syringe extrusions and finish as described.

You could make a 3 dimension sculptural piece using this project as a starting point. Follow the instructions through step 4. Then use a rolled clay slab to create organic shapes like leaves, flower petals, etc. or make a geometric design and texture it with rubber stamps or brass plates. Let your imagination go wild.

Using PMC3 paste, secure the dimensional parts to the dry glass and syringe work. You can form flowers or sculptural shapes to give your work a more complex 3D design.

Dichroic Glass and Fine Silver Brooch

Silver Painting on Glass

Using PMC3 Paste as a Painting Medium on Glass
By Mary Ann Devos

PMC3 paste is an excellent medium to use in a painterly manner on glass. We have used it to enhance glass cabochons with reliable success. You can also use commercially produced glass items like perfume bottles, dresser trays and other small items. However, be aware that 3D glass objects will distort at the firing temperature used for this surface decoration process.

Materials & Equipment

PMC3 paste
Glass object: e.g. perfume bottle, cabochon, pendant, small tray, etc.

Small artist's brush
Stainless steel wire brush
Burnishing tool
Soap and water (for glass cleaning)
Programmable kiln
Fiberboard kiln shelf

Mary Ann Devos, "Petroglyphs"
Photo: Ken Devos

Procedure:

1. We used PMC+ for the first project in this chapter but in that project the silver clay was already fired before it was added to the glass. The second project used PMC3 to decorate the glass but the firing temperature of 1110°F / 600°C matured the silver but did not soften the glass. For this project we will take the firing temperature high enough to soften the glass enabling the silver and glass to bond permanently. To avoid stressing the glass and possibly causing it to break, it is important to keep the PMC3 layer very thin.

2. Thoroughly clean the glass object that you have chosen to decorate.

3. Thin the PMC3 paste slightly. Paint a free form pattern or use a stencil to copy a design onto the glass. Let the paste dry, then add a second thin layer and dry it again or use a fine syringe extrusion to decorate the glass.

4. Fire the piece in a programmable kiln using the slow-fire schedule with a hold temperature of 1200°F / 650°C and the hold time at 20 minutes. The slow-fire schedule will set a ramp-up speed (increase in temperature) of 1500°F/ 816°C per hour. In other words it will take about 45 minutes to reach the hold temperature of 1200°F / 650°C. This ramp-up speed is adequate for small jewelry sized objects less than 3" (7.6 cm) diameter. Larger pieces will require a very slow ramp-up rate (see Garnish Dish project, page 29 step 9). When the firing is finished open the door open to crash cool to 950°F / 537°C.

5. Cool slowly after firing. Just turn off the kiln off and allow it to cool until it is at room temperature.

6. Polish the silver with a stainless steel brush and bring to a high shine using a burnishing tool.

Observations & Alternatives

It is not necessary to use fusing compatible glass for this technique however it is important to follow proper ramp up, annealing and cool down procedures for the size and type of glass object that you are using. For example, larger glass items will require a slower ramp up and a longer annealing period than smaller items.

When glass reaches 1200°F / 650°C it softens enabling the silver to bond to the glass permanently. However, at this temperature a 3D object will slump and distort. This element of surprise can add interest to the final piece.

For more information on the art of glass fusing we recommend a book by Petra Kaiser 'Introduction to Glass Fusing' ISBN: 919985-38-6 published by Wardell Publications Inc.

Silver Painting on a Glass Object

Chapter 2
PMC and Enamel

Enamel is a wonderful way to allow color to become an integral part of the overall project design. Enamel artists recognized the benefits of PMC almost from the very introduction of the material.

Mary Ann Devos, "Egypt On My Mind"
Photo: Ken Devos

Mary Ann Devos, "Green Defender"
Photo: Ken Devos

Mary Ann Devos, "Flutterby"
Photo: Ken Devos

34 Chapter 2 – Precious Metal Clay and Enamel

Linda Bernstein, "Celtic Bracelet"
Photo: Rob Stegmann

Mary Ann Devos, "Happy House"
Photo: Ken Devos

Enamel On PMC

PMC provides a vibrant textural base that enhances the intensity of transparent enamel colors.

Leslie Tieke,
"Blue In The Face"
Photo: Rob Stegmann

Chapter 2 - Precious Metal Clay and Enamel

Leslie Tieke, "Purple Hearts"
Photo: Rob Stegmann

Leslie Tieke, "Dreams and Streams" *Photo: Rob Stegmann*

Enamel On PMC

Leslie Tieke,
"Tears and Passion"
Photo: Rob Stegmann

36 Chapter 2 - Precious Metal Clay and Enamel

PMC Silver and Enamel Moonstar Pendant

Using PMC Silver and Colored Enamels
By Leslie Tieke

The Moonstar necklace is a project that is sure to bring enjoyment as you allow your creativity to mingle among the stars. Turn your celestial dreams into fine silver! In this project, you will have fun adding color to silver, through the application of enamels.

Materials & Equipment

PMC+ lump
PMC+ syringe
PMC+ Paste
Thompson Enamels
   (your choice of colors)
Glass and silver beads
Silver wire - 20 gauge
Silver or sterling findings
Enameling tools
   fork, spoon - small
   sifter – small, trivet
   wire rack
PVC slab-roller
Brass texture sheet
Craft knife
Needle tool
Round nose pliers
Emery board
Stainless steel wire brush
Rotary tumbler with
   stainless steel shot
Programmable kiln
Fiberboard kiln shelf

Procedure:

1. Make a full-size sketch of the star and moon design (or other design).

2. Place PMC+ onto a brass texture sheet and use the PVC roller and thickness slats to roll out a medium thick slab (see page 15). Place your sketch on top of the clay slab, trace the outline with the needle tool and cut out the clay shape. Do this for both shapes.

3. Use a small bit of clay to roll a thin rope of clay. Cut two 1" (2.5 cm) lengths and form each into a loop. Attach one loop to the top of the star and the other to the top of the moon. Attach the loop to the slab at the loop joints. (This is where findings will be attached.)

Leslie Tieke, "Moonstar" Photo: Leslie Tieke

4. Use the syringe to create a border of clay along the outside edge of the star and moon. Add your own design on the interior of the star and moon creating cells where the enamels will be packed.

5. Allow the pieces to thoroughly dry, then gently clean all the rough edges using an emery board.

6. Fire pieces in your kiln at 1470°F/ 800°C degrees for 30 minutes.

7. Polish the white surface of the cooled pieces with your stainless steel brush and place in rotary tumbler with mixed stainless steel shot and burnishing solution for 20 to 30 minutes.

8. Place a small amount of each enamel color in its own small plastic cup. Wash the enamels by running water into the cup, wait a few seconds and pour off the residue that will be floating on top. Repeat this rinse step 3 to 4 times until the water remains clean.

9. Make sure your piece is clean. We will start by applying a counter enamel. Place the pieces on the enamel trivet and sift one color of dry enamel evenly on the back surface of your star and moon. You can dry the enamel by placing a small amount on a piece of aluminum foil and place it in a warm area.

10. Pre-heat kiln to 1450°F / 788°C. Place the pieces including the trivet into the hot kiln using the enameling fork. The kiln will lose heat when placing your piece inside, so allow the kiln to come back up to 1450°F / 788°C. Leave the piece inside the kiln for two to three minutes and remove them from the kiln only when the enamels look glassy and wet. Set them aside and allow to cool.

11. Gently pack the enamels in the chosen cell design areas. This is called the "wet pack" technique. Take the time to pack the enamels in a thin even layer on the silver. Repeat firing process in step 10. Place additional thin enamels as need to achieve the intensity of color that you are looking for. Be sure to keep the enamel below the level of the silver cell wall.

12. Burnish the desired exposed areas of PMC, to create a shiny contrast to the enamels. Use jewelry pliers and sterling or fine silver wire to add beadwork and findings as desired.

Observations & Alternatives

If you don't want to counter enamel (the back side) make a thicker PMC slab 5/64" (2 mm). Counter enameling or a thick slab will prevent the enamel layer from cracking or crazing over time.

This is a very simplified example of a complex artform. We hope this introduction to enameling encourages you to explore this medium further. You will find many fine books and instructors on this subject to guide you.

Chapter 2 - Precious Metal Clay and Enamel

Enamel In PMC

In addition to placing enamels on PMC, we also have the ability to place enamels in PMC. Mixing PMC and enamel powder creates a hybrid material with the solidness of metal colored by enamel. The results can be striking, from very subtle shades to vibrant hues.

Mary Ellin D'Agostino, "Iris Pin"
Photo: Rob Stegmann

Mary Ellin D'Agostino, "Squares"
Photo: Rob Stegmann

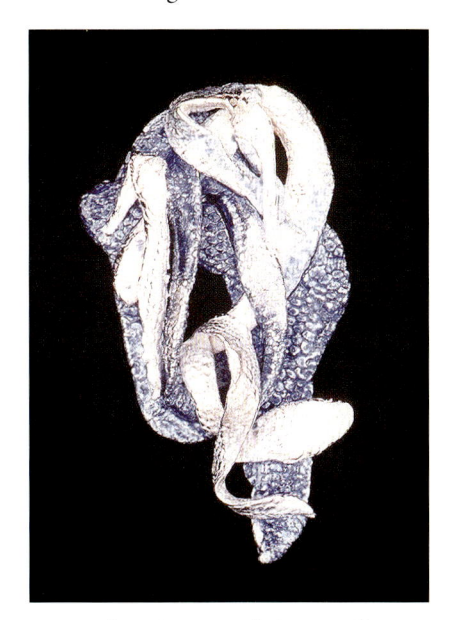

Mary Ellin D'Agostino, "Blue Swirl"
Photo: Rob Stegmann

Mary Ellin D'Agostino "Morning Orchid"
Photo: Ken Devos

Mary Ellin D'Agostino, "Waves"
Photo: Rob Stegmann

Mary Ellin D'Agostino
Photo: Ken Devos

Enamel In PMC

PMC Silver and Enamel Wave Earrings

Mixing the Enamel Directly into the PMC3 Clay
By Mary Ellin D'Agostino

What is really new is the potential for mixing the enamel directly into the PMC3 and firing it to create a hybrid material. While this method is faster and less fussy than traditional enameling techniques, the color range is somewhat limited. It's easy to do and you can get fantastic results.

Materials & Equipment

PMC3 clay
PMC3 paste
Earring loops
Thinfire separator paper
Freezer or Teflon paper
Thompson Enamels in three or more of the following colors:
Cobalt blue (1685), Gem green (2325), Turquoise (2435), Prussian blue (2680)

Small artist's brush
Pallet knife – small
Hair dryer
Stainless steel wire brush
Burnishing tool
Programmable kiln
Fiberboard kiln shelf

Mary Ellin D'Agostino, "Waves II"
Photo: Rob Stegmann

Procedure:

1. Decide on the basic shape you want for your project and draw the design full-size on a piece of paper. The earrings we are making are the same for left and right however, if your design requires mirror images you should create a reverse drawing for the second earring.

2. Choose the enamel colors you want to use. Measure out 1/16th teaspoon of your first enamel color onto a clean sheet of paper. If the smallest measure spoon you have is 1/4 tsp, simply place the pile on a paper and use a palette knife to cut the pile into quarters and return the extra enamel to the jar. Clean the palette knife and repeat this for all colors in the project, using a separate sheet of paper for each color.

3. Be careful to not mix the enamel colors. The ratio of clay to enamel should be equal amounts of clay to enamel for full saturation of the enamel color. If you want to get a lighter effect simply cut back on the enamel amount.

4. Transfer the colored enamels from the plain paper onto the parchment paper or plastic sheet for mixing. Dip the paintbrush into water and just touch the brush to the enamel to moisten it. Do this for each color, but be sure that the brush is clean between adding water to each color.

5. Take 10 grams of PMC3 and divide it into 5 equal balls of clay. Cover them all with plastic wrap so they don't dry out while you are working.

6. Thoroughly mix one ball PMC into each color of enamel using the palette knife. You can add more water as necessary to facilitate mixing. Be sure to clean the palette knife between mixing each color to avoid contaminating the enamel colors.

7. Allow the clay and enamel mixtures to dry (if necessary) until you can shape the enamel and clay mixture into a ball that you can roll in your hands. Split each ball in half (one for each earring). Remember to wear gloves if you are not positive your enamels are lead-free (see safety).

8. At this point, you should have 8 balls of clay: 2 plain balls and 2 of each of the three colors.

9. Roll a ball of clay of the first color into matching coils and place on the patterns. While they do not have to match exactly, a good match will enhance the appearance of your earrings.

10. Repeat for other colored mixtures and the plain PMC3 clay. When rolling out and applying the plain PMC3 clay, roll out one end a little thinner. As you apply this final piece to the design, use the extra, thinner part of the coil to create a bail. Use paste to join the end to the coil. An alternative is to punch a hole with a small straw to enable you to attach the sterling findings.

11. Gently compress the pieces together, applying a small amount of water and paste to ensure that the coils bond together. Apply texture if desired using rubber stamps, textured paper, lace or with potters tools.

12. Dry the piece thoroughly in a dryer box or with the hair dryer.

13. Twist stainless steel wire into a frame for suspending the earrings over the kiln shelf. If you lay the pieces directly on the kiln shelf, they may stick or have rough backs.

14. Fire at 1450°F / 788°C for 10 minutes. PMC and enamel mixtures should generally be fired starting with a cool kiln. Note: PMC+ can be used for this technique but the extended firing temperature and time degrade the colors in the enamels.

15. Brush and polish the silver surfaces of the piece as usual. Finish by attaching the beads and earring wires.

Enamel Wave Earrings

Observations & Alternatives

Safety First:

Thompson and other enamels made in the United States are lead free. If you are using older enamels or those from France or Japan, they may contain lead and you should take precautions to avoid the health hazards associated with lead—wear gloves and a dust mask when handling these types of enamels. All enamels create a dust that is a hazard to breathe. Always wear a dust mask when working with dry enamels and work with good ventilation.

Blues and greens are really the only colors of enamel that work well when mixed into PMC. Most other colors of enamels can't take the sustained heat and usually turn a khaki color. If you want to add touches of other colors to your piece, you can mix them with water [or Klyr-fire] and apply them using the wet pack method similar to the Moonstar project on page 37.

The mixture ratios given here provide a full saturation of the clay with color. Subdue the color intensity by decreasing the amount of enamel that is mixed into the clay.

Chapter 3
PMC and Polymer Clay

Another way to add color to PMC is the use of polymer clay. The introduction of polymer clay and its success within the art and craft markets were major reasons for the development of PMC into these same markets. Now we can use them together to take advantage of their combined benefits. Polymer clay provides an element of color. PMC contributes the value of precious metal. Combined they have the potential for heirloom quality jewelry.

Linda Bernstein, "Goddess"
Photo: Larry Sanders

Linda Bernstein, "Helping Hand"
Photo: Rob Stegmann

Leslie Tieke, "Micro Mosaic"
Photo: Rob Stegmann

42   Chapter 3 - Precious Metal Clay and Polymer Clay

Linda Bernstein, "Geometric Burst"
Photo: Rob Stegmann

Chapter 3
PMC and Polymer Clay

Linda Bernstein, "Japur Rose"
Photo: Larry Sanders

Linda Bernstein, "Upbeat Elephant"
Photo: Rob Stegmann

Chapter 3 - Precious Metal Clay and Polymer Clay 43

PMC And Polymer Clay Art Earrings

Vibrant Colors Add Charisma to Silver Jewelry
By Linda Bernstein

Polymer clay art has experienced a tremendous increase in popularity in recent years expanding its role from simple craft into the sphere of fine art. The similar working characteristics and relative popularity of both PMC and polymer clay make these 2 materials a logical choice to use in combination.

Materials & Equipment

PMC+ clay
PMC+ syringe
PMC+ paste
Polymer clay
CZ's (optional)

PVC roller
Texture plate
Stainless steel wire brush
Burnishing tool
Programmable kiln
Fiberboard kiln shelf

What is Polymer Clay?

Polymer clay is made by suspending grains of polyvinyl chloride (PVC) in plasticizer material that creates a material that can be shaped and used very much like potters earthenware clay but doesn't dry out until it is oven-cured. Available in dozens of colors that can be mixed, blended and integrated in countless combinations to create colorful patterns from mosaic to millefiori style designs.

Procedure:

1. Place 1/4 of one package of PMC+ lump clay (about 4.5 grams) on a lightly oiled textured plate and roll a medium thick slab (see pg 15).

2. Gently peel the slab off the texture plate and place it texture side up on piece of parchment paper. Create 2 interesting shapes for the outer boundary using a clay-stamp cutter, a cookie cutter or a craft knife.

3. Use a smaller cutter or the craft knife to cut and remove an interior pattern. In the case of the earrings shown above, we made a flat ring shape (like a donut). See photo on page 45 at top.

4. Next create a coil (see pg 16) from the remaining half of the PMC clay. Use the roll-plate to form a 3/32" (2.4 mm) diameter coil.

Linda Bernstein, "Ringed Earrings" Photo: Ken Devos

5. Shape the coil around the inner edge of the hole in the slab form. Use some paste between the coil and the slab for a secure joint. This coil around the inner edge is called a 'locking gap' and will be used later to position the polymer clay insert.

6. Finish by adding decorative touches to the clay using various texturing tools or use the syringe to add some appliqué styling. You could also incorporate CZ's. Use a small plastic drinking straw to punch a light hole wherever you want to place one. Then use the syringe to extrude a collar around the light hole high enough to capture the girdle of the stone. See 'Stone setting with PMC' on page 18 for more details on this process.

7. Dry the piece completely using a hand held hair dryer, a drying box or a dehydrator (see pg 19-20).

8. Fire in a programmable kiln at 1650°F / 900°C for 10 minutes (see pg 21 for firing Procedure).

9. When the piece is cool, polish the surface with a stainless steel brush for a matte finish or give it a shiny surface using a burnishing tool or the rotary tumbler with mixed stainless steel shot (see pg 22-23).

Polymer Clay

10. Create a design from the polymer clay that is the correct size and shape to fill the opening in your silver jewelry piece. Use standard PMC shaping techniques to work this soft and flexible material into a multicolored design with textures, swirls or any number of features. The fired polymer clay is quite hard and durable and can be refined in various ways to resemble glass, stone, terracotta, marble, semi-precious stones and many other effects.

11. When your polymer shape is complete, set it into the open space of your finished silver item and gently force mold it into the locking gap.

12. Place the finished piece into a cold oven and set a temperature from 250°F to 275°F (120°C to 135°C). When it reaches optimum firing temperature, soak for 20 minutes then turn the oven off and let it cool. Polymer clay can be fired in a standard kitchen oven, a countertop toaster oven or a convection oven (but not a microwave oven). It is important to use an oven thermometer to ensure the temperature in the oven is accurate because the clay will burn if exposed to temperatures of 300°F (177°C) or higher.

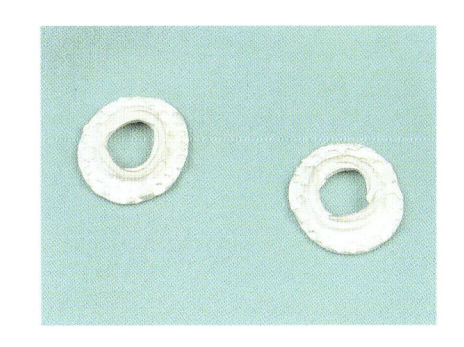

Observations & Alternatives

Silver Inlays

Instead of adding polymer to a PMC item you could add a pure silver highlight to a polymer sculpture. Create your PMC add-in item, dry it, fire it and finish in the normal way. Now create your polymer sculpture and gently press the PMC highlight item into the soft polymer clay. Bake the polymer in the oven and when it has cooled pop the silver out of the polymer and reset it using E-6000, 2 part epoxy or other suitable adhesive.

Polymer Clay Art Earrings

One of the most appealing ways to add color to PMC pieces is to use pure gold. The combination of these two precious metals elevates the finished pieces to a new level of appeal. Even a small amount of gold creates an increased desirability in the marketplace.

Chapter 4
PMC Silver and Gold

Mary Ann Devos, "Ebb and Flow"
Photo: Rob Stegmann

Mary Ellin D'Agostino, "Royal Starch"
Photo: Rob Stegmann

Mary Ann Devos, & Lisa Roberts
"Rapted Attention"
Photo: Ken Devos

46   Chapter 4 - PMC Silver and 22K Gold

Chapter 4
PMC Silver and Gold

Mary Ann Devos, "She Sells..." Photo: Ken Devos

Mary Ann Devos, "Golden Happiness" Photo: Ken Devos

There are many ways to add gold to PMC pieces. Artists use PMC Gold, as a solid clay inclusion element or as gold paste, to enhance the surface of the silver. The paste method is my favorite, extending the number of pieces I can adorn with gold. Another way is the ancient Korean technique called Keum Boo, where gold foil is bonded to the silver.

Mary Ann Devos, "Donora Bead" Photo: Ken Devos

Mary Ann Devos, "Sea Basket" Photo: Rob Stegmann

Chapter 4 - PMC Silver and Gold

PMC Gold Highlights on a Silver Pendant

Use Gold Paste to Add Intensity to Silver Jewelry
By Mary Ann Devos

We have been experimenting with a gold paste that we mix up ourselves using distilled water and PMC 22K Gold Clay. We've run many test firings in a kiln as well as with a torch and have concluded that torch firing provides the best result. The fired pieces can be finished with a stainless steel brush and burnisher but our rotary tumbler produces a brilliant gold shine that is very exciting.

Materials & Equipment

PMC+ or PMC3 piece, formed and finished to the bone-dry stage
PMC Gold – lump clay

Small artist's brush
Tweezers
Stainless steel wire brush
Burnishing tool
Butane torch & Fuel
Fiberboard kiln shelf

Mary Ann Devos, "Flutterby"
Photo: Ken Devos

Procedure:

1. Mix 1 or 2 grams of PMC Gold clay with enough distilled water to make a loose paste the consistency of heavy cream (or thin yogurt). I cleaned out an old PMC silver paste jar and use that for my gold paste. Make sure to mark it accordingly.

2. Create a pendant, a ring, earrings or anything you would like using either PMC+ or PMC3. Dry and finish the piece to the bone-dry (aka greenware) stage.

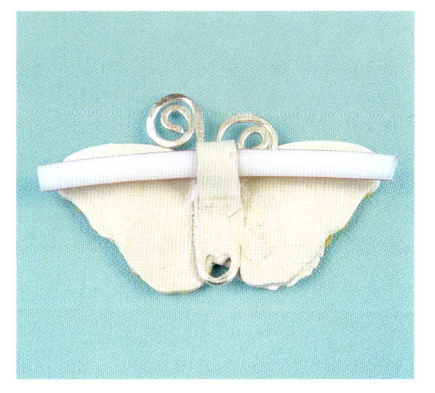

3. Use the small artist's brush to apply 2 to 4 thin coats of the gold paste to areas on the silver greenware that you want gold. Since the silver piece is bone-dry the moisture is absorbed immediately making it a bit tricky to spread the gold paste. That is why we recommend using a thin gold paste mixture to apply 2 to 4 coats rather than try to lay the gold paste down in one thicker coat.

4. Dry the piece completely (see pg 19-20) and make any necessary refinements in the bone-dry state.

5. We are now ready to fire the piece. It is possible to fire the piece in a kiln, however we seem to get better results using the butane torch and following the same firing procedure as for PMC+. Here are the basic steps. Place your dried clay piece on the kiln shelf. Ignite the torch, following the manufacturer's directions and adjust the fuel flow until the inner blue flame is about 1-1/2" (4 cm) long. Aim the inner flame slightly above the piece you are firing to warm it, then slowly move the flame closer to increase the intensity of the heat being applied.

6. Move the torch in circular motion keeping the flame continuously in motion across the entire piece. Bring the piece to an orange glow and hold that temperature for 4 to 5 minutes (for a 10-gram piece). Be careful not to overheat the piece because you can actually melt it. If the surface turns from orange to a shimmering "wet-looking" silver color, immediately move the torch farther away from the piece to reduce the heat. The shimmering look indicates the surface is starting to melt.

7. After the piece is fired and cooled, do an initial polish with a stainless steel wire brush. Put the final touch for a shine with the burnishing tool or place it in a rotary tumbler with stainless steel mixed shot for an overall shiny surface.

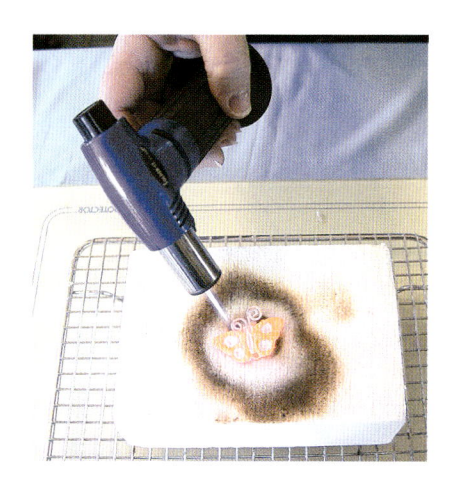

Observations & Alternatives

It is possible to add gold to an already fired silver piece. First apply a coat of PMC3 paste where you want to add the gold. Then apply the gold paste over the PMC3 paste. Dry and fire with the torch as described in this project.

Gold Highlights on a Silver Pendant

PMC Gold Stamped Earrings

Use PMC Gold Lump Clay to Make 22K Solid Gold Jewelry
By Mary Ann Devos

The previous project presented a simple way to use PMC Gold in paste form to enhance silver PMC+ or PMC3 pieces. For this project we will build solid PMC gold earrings. 22K PMC Gold has lower firing temperatures than the original PMC Gold, firing criteria very similar to PMC silver. These provide a greater range of use options than were possible using the original PMC Gold.

Materials & Equipment

PMC Gold clay
Earring findings
 (14K gold wire hooks)

Small artist's brush
PVC roller
Rubber stamp
Texture plate
Drying device
Stainless steel wire brush
Programmable kiln
Fiberboard kiln shelf

Mary Ann Devos, "Calusa Mask Earrings" Photo: Ken Devos

Procedure:

1 Open the PMC Gold lump clay package and take out 5 grams. Roll it between your palms to create a ball and place it on a lightly oiled textured plate. Flatten the ball slightly then use the PVC roller to create a very thin slab that is approximately 1/64" (.5 mm). We are safe to make this gold slab thinner than we would for silver because PMC gold is a stronger material. (See pg 15 for slab rolling details).

2. Gently press the rubber stamp into the PMC gold clay. I used a Calusa Indian design rubber stamp for my earrings but any small patterned rubber stamp will work.

3. Use a craft knife, a clay-stamp cutter or a small cookie cutter (round, star shape, heart shape, etc.) to create two earrings of the same size and shape from the gold clay slab. Be careful to reclaim every speck of cutaway clay. Gather it up and combine it with any gold clay remaining in the package. Thoroughly wrap it in plastic and store it in a zip lock bag.

4. Moisten the artist's brush and smooth the edges of the earring to remove any sharp or pointed areas.

5. Use a toothpick or a small plastic stirring straw to punch a hole near the top of each earring. This hole will be used to insert the earring wire loops.

6. Use your favorite drying device to dry the pieces completely (see pg 19-20).

7. When the piece is bone-dry use emery board and/or needle file to refine the shape and surface.

8. Place the earrings in the programmable kiln and set the schedule to fire the piece at piece at one of the temperature/time schedules shown in the firing charts. (See pages 8 or 21.)

9. When the pieces are removed from the kiln the surface will be an earthy matte orange color. PMC Gold needs to be brushed and burnish (same as the silver) to polish the surface. This can be accomplished either by hand or in a rotary tumbler.

10. Finish the earrings by attaching 14K gold earring findings.

Observations & Alternatives

The fabrication process for PMC Gold is very similar to creating with PMC+ silver clay. In fact, PMC Gold has a shrinkage factor slightly greater the PMC+ (14% to 19% vs 12%) that must be taken into consideration when you are designing your gold jewelry pieces.

Because PMC Gold is 22K gold, it is important to conserve every single speck of the clay both before and after firing. Any dust created in smoothing the bone-dry pieces should be gathered and placed in a separate container, such as a 35 mm film canister. Since there may be foreign items such as grit from sandpaper in this dust, it is better to use this reclaimed gold dust to make gold paste rather than to try to combine it with the unused gold clay.

Gold PMC Stamped Earrings

Keum Boo Gold Foil Technique

Add Gold Accents using an Ancient Korean Technique
By Mary Ann Devos

Keum Boo is an ancient Korean metal working technique that enables artists to add stunning gold accents to PMC Standard, PMC+ or PMC3 pieces. Gold foil in 22K or 24K will fuse to fine silver at temperatures of 650°F to 950°F (345°C to 510°C). The method produces a permanent fused bond between the gold foil and the silver and is accomplished using a decidedly low-tech but very effective method.

Materials & Equipment

PMC Standard, PMC+ or PMC3 piece, formed, fired and finished.

Gold foil in 22K or 24K

Klyr Fire (a temporary adhesive) manufactured by Thompson Enamels

Small artist's brush
Long Tweezers (12")
Burnishing tool - agate
Heat resistant gloves
Fine soldering screen or small brass plate
Fiberboard kiln shelf (as safe work surface)
Hot plate - any brand with high, medium and low settings

Procedure:

1. Form, fire and finish a PMC Standard, PMC+ or PMC3 jewelry item that has a smooth or lightly textured area to receive the gold foil application. Leave the areas where you intend to place the gold highlights with the white matte surface created in the firing process.. This will enable the two metals to fuse properly.

Mary Ann Devos, "Stonehenge"
Photo: Ken Devos

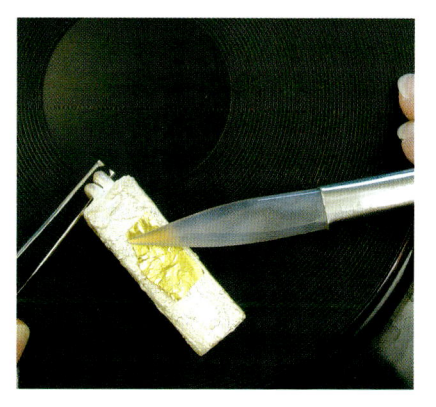

2. The hot plate that we use has a solid element burner (the black surface in the center photo above is the burner). If you want to use a hot plate with an exposed 'coil type' heating element, place a sheet of brass or copper on the element as a work surface. Turn the hot plate to medium-high setting to pre-heat.

3. Cut the gold foil into the shapes necessary to fit the areas you want to accent.

4. Use the artist's brush to apply Klyr Fire to an area, apply the gold foil and gently press down to secure it. Klyr Fire is a temporary adhesive used to hold the gold foil in place. During the heat bonding process the Klyr Fire will dissipate without affecting the metals. Glue all gold foil pieces to your work as desired.

5. Use heat resistant gloves and long tweezers to place your project piece on the hot plate. The metal must reach at least 650°F / 345°C for the metals to begin to fuse. After heating it for a minute or so touch an area of gold foil with the tip of an agate burnishing tool to test if the fusing has begun. Watch for the gold foil color to brighten up and smooth out easily under the burnisher tool. When this occurs, gently rub and smooth the gold foil to help it bond to the silver. Periodically cool the burnisher by dipping it in water to prevent the gold from sticking to the burnisher.

6. Repeat this process for all areas that have gold foil until you have obtained the results you are looking for.

7. Turn off the hot plate and move the finished piece to a heat resistant surface to let it cool.

8. Finish the surface by hand polishing with a soft jeweler's cloth only. The gold is very thin and will show wear and tear if subjected to heavy polishing or constant use (sorry, can't use the rotary tumbler this time). For best long-term results plan your design to place the gold in recesses and areas that will be protected from wear.

Observations & Alternatives

Gold foil may be a bit difficult to obtain. It is easily confused with the gold leaf, which is too thin, or gold sheet which is too thick for this process. Gold foil has limited availability but is available from PMC Connection distributors.

PMC Gold paste and Keum Boo gold foiling are effective ways to enhance your pieces with gold. Another option is to embed 24K gold casting grains or 24K jewelry wire as inclusions into your silver items. 24K gold findings are available from jewelry suppliers and come in a wide variety of shapes and sizes. Casting grains can be set into the wet silver clay and capture in the same method as gemstones. Gold and silver does not bond sufficiently to hold the two metals together permanently. Make sure to fully embed the gold grain or gold wire into the silver clay or use the syringe clay to form a silver net to hold the gold in place.

Yet another method is to use 18K gold wire and wire wrapping techniques to capture your silver creations. Examine the pendant on page 46, bottom right, as an example.

Keum Boo Gold Foil Technique

The clay-like nature of PMC in its raw form begs for its use together with ceramic clay. Since most types of ceramic clay mature at a much higher temperature than PMC, we usually work with already fired ceramic pieces. We can combine PMC with bisque (low fired) ceramics, high fired, glazed or even unfired clay as long as the clay shrinkage rates and firing temperatures are compatible with those of the PMC. All items shown here used already fired ceramics.

Chapter 5
PMC and Ceramics

Mary Ann Devos & Marlynda Taylor,
"Moon Pot" Photo: Ken Devos

Vera Lightstone, "Natural Leaf Bottle"
Photo: Rob Stegmann

Tonya Davidson, "Arizona Confections"
Photo: Rob Stegmann

Chapter 5
PMC and Ceramics

Helen & Dick Tickal, "Victorian Doll"
Photo: Ken Devos

Vera Lightstone, "Chalice"
Photo: Rob Stegmann

Vera Lightstone, "Parallel"
Photo: Rob Stegmann

Chapter 5 - Precious Metal Clay and Ceramics 55

PMC Adornments for Fine Porcelain Dolls

The Perfect Complement to Finely Crafted Porcelain Dolls
By Mary Ann Devos

Fine porcelain dolls with very exquisite outfits deserve the adornment of fine silver, one-of-a-kind jewelry. This can be accomplished by firing the jewelry decorations directly onto the porcelain dolls before they are assembled or make small scale accessories separately, then place them on the doll. Helen and Dick Tickal made the beautiful Victorian doll that I am using as an example for this project.

Materials & Equipment

PMC+ sheet
PMC3 paste
PMC3 syringe
Cubic zirconia stones
Porcelain doll
Paper and pencil

Decorative paper punch
Small artist's brush
Tweezers
Drying device
Fiberglass bristle brush
Agate burnishing tool
Programmable kiln
Fiberboard kiln shelf

Helen & Dick Tickal, "Victorian Doll"
Photo: Ken Devos

Procedure:

1. Cut decorative pattern pieces from the sheet type clay. Use an ornamental paper punch to create the jewelry components or draw a custom necklace and earring design on a piece of paper and cut your design using scissors or a craft knife.

2. The porcelain doll component must be finished, glazed and fired. Use a small artist's brush to paint the back of each sheet clay cutout with PMC3 paste. This PMC paste will hold your pieces to the doll until it is fired and will fuse to the doll during firing.

3. Carefully arrange the PMC+ sheet cutouts on the dolls neck, back, arm or hand, as your design requires. Check to ensure the pieces are firmly attached. Add more paste if necessary but remember the paste is silver and will leave silver wherever you use the paste.

4. Use your favorite drying device to dry the pieces completely (see page 19-20). The paste will dry but the sheet will remain soft even when it is bone-dry.

5. When the components are dry you can add CZ's if desired. Use the ultra fine tip on a PMC3 syringe to make bezel extrusion rings, then press the CZ's into the bezels making sure that the girdle of the stone is fully captured. Finish the jewelry using the syringe with ultra fine tip to create neck chain links, bracelet bands or many other jewelry components.

6. Place the porcelain doll parts in the programmable kiln and set the firing schedule to a slow ramp up speed of 1500°F/ 815°C per hour. Fire to 1470°F / 800°C for 30 minutes. After firing, turn the kiln off and allow it to cool slowly to prevent thermal shock to the porcelain.

7. After the piece is fired and cooled, do an initial polish with a fiberglass bristle brush to burnish the surface of the silver. Finish with an agate burnishing tool to add shine and highlights.

Note: Do not use a stainless steel or brass brush or a steel burnisher as these tools will mark the porcelain surface.

Helen & Dick Tickal are internationally recognized Master Doll Artists and instructors. They design and create fine porcelain dolls, specializing in period costuming. They have exhibited their work and have won multiple awards at major shows and competitions both internationally and throughout the USA.

Observations & Alternatives

The jewelry can be fired in place before the doll is completed (as we did in this project) or it could be made to scale, fired and polished and then attached to the doll during doll assembly using fine silver wire, fine chain or epoxy adhesive.

PMC Adornments for Fine Porcelain Dolls

PMC Silver Coated Bisque Fired Beads
Ceramic Beads Covered with Fine Silver
By Tonya Davidson

For some people hand forming many fine silver beads in the same size and shape or in complementary sizes and shapes for use in a necklace can be more effort than they desire. This technique, using bisque fired, non-glazed ceramic beads as the base shape, provides a simple solution.

Materials & Equipment

PMC3 paste
   (one container makes
   about 15-20 beads)
PMC3 syringe
PMC+ sheet
   (for embellishing)
Bisque Bead Blanks
Cubic zirconia stones
Casting grains -
   fine silver or 24K gold

Small artist's brush
Chenille pipe cleaners
Styrofoam block
Drying device
Stainless steel wire brush
Burnishing tool or Rotary
   tumbler with mixed
   stainless steel shot
Programmable kiln
Fiber blanket or kiln
   bar-stilts and Nichrome
   wire armatures

Tonya Davidson, "Eye Candies"
Photo: Rob Stegmann

Procedure:

1. Prepare the surface of the bisque bead by sanding with fine emery cloth or an emery board to remove imperfections. Clean and remove dust with a damp sponge.

2. String each bead separately on a length of chenille pipe cleaner. To keep the bead from moving around while painting, fold over the end of your pipe cleaner and insert this doubled over end into the bead.

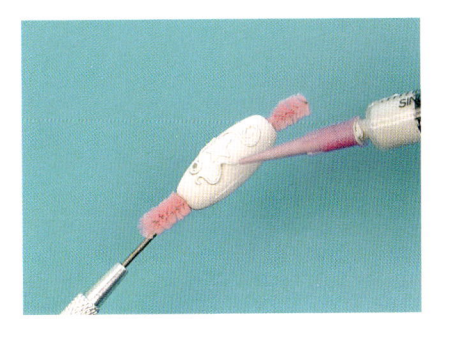

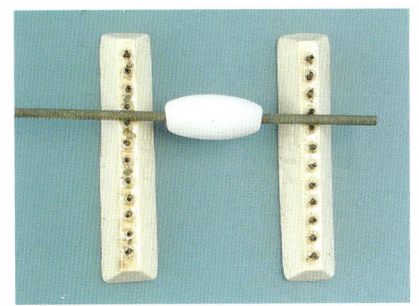

3. Use a small artist's brush to paint the bisque beads with the PMC3 paste. It's best to start at the ends first, coating over the edge and down into of the hole of the bead. When you have the first coat on stick the end of the pipe cleaner into the styrofoam block to let the bead dry. Now put the first coat on the next bead and continue until all beads are coated once. One container of PMC3 pate will make about 15-20 beads (depending on bead size).

4. Continue to apply successive coats of paste to the beads until you have 5-6 coats total on each bead. Make sure to coat approximately 1/16" (1.6 mm) down inside the holes.

5. Place the beads into your drying device to dry completely.

6. Use 800-1000 grit sandpaper to gently sand each bead to remove brush strokes and smooth the surface of the bead. This smooth surface will make it much easier to achieve a mirror finish. Be careful not to sand off too much of the silver paste. If you prefer a satin finish 4 coats of paste will be adequate and you can skip the sanding step

7. At this stage you should add embellishments such as syringe work, CZ's, lab grown stones or shapes made from pre-fired PMC sheet.

8. Put the beads in the programmable kiln. Protect the surface by placing them on a fiber blanket or string them on Nichrome wire armatures supported by bar-stilts (see photo at top right). You should be able to place 20 or more beads in each kiln load, all on one shelf.

9. Set the firing schedule to a slow ramp up speed of 1500°F/ 815°C per hour. This ramp up will take approximately 1 hour 6 minutes to get to the final firing temperature of to 1650°F / 900°C. Hold this temperature for 10 minutes. After holding, turn the kiln off and allow it to cool slowly to prevent thermal shock to the ceramic beads.

10. After the beads are fired and cooled, do an initial polish with a stainless steel wire brush. Put the final touch for a shine with the burnishing tool or place it in a rotary tumbler with stainless steel mixed shot. Tumbling tip: place the pipe cleaner back into bead and curl over each end to prevent shot from getting stuck in the bead. Tumble with burnishing fluid for 20 minutes to get an overall mirror-shiny finish.

PMC Silver Coated Bisque Fired Beads

Observations & Alternatives

After firing, you may discover some areas where the ceramic bead is showing through the silver. This is easily repaired by adding more paste and re-firing. With experience you will discover how heavily to apply the product and to ensure the entire bead gets covered with each coat.

It's fun to add embellishments to these beads (see step 7). Use the fine tip syringe to extrude a bezel to set small CZ's or lab-grown stones. Tip: to flush mount a stone for a 'deep-set' appearance, pre-drill a small pocket in the bead using a high-speed rotary tool. Set the stone down into hole and extrude a syringe bezel around the top.

Punch or cut fancy design shapes from sheet clay to use for embellishing. Pre-fire the sheet stampings to maintain their pure shape and make them easier to apply to the bead. Use tweezers to hold the pre-fired shape, coat it with paste clay and then press it firmly onto the bead. Sheet shapes can be pre-fired quickly with a Butane torch.

You can also add PMC embellishments to glazed beads. The process is the same except you must stilt these beads on the Nichrome wire armatures to prevent the glaze from sticking.

Stoneware Plate with Silver Figure

Using Painter's Techniques To Apply Paste Clay As A Medium
By Vera Lightstone

When PMC was originally under development, Mitsubishi researchers consulted several noted Japanese potters to ascertain the best consistency for molding and forming. Traditional ceramic clay and modern silver clay are unrelated materials but with some creative ingenuity can work collectively, each type enhancing the role of the other.

Materials & Equipment

PMC+ or PMC3 paste
Ceramic item, glazed and fired (this project uses a small ceramic tray)
Drawing paper
Transfer paper

Small artist's brush
Drying device
Fiberglass bristle brush
Burnishing tool
Jeweler's polishing cloth
Liver of sulfur (optional for patina)
Programmable kiln
Fiberboard kiln shelf

Vera Lightstone, "Reclining Nude"
Photo: Ken Devos

Chapter 5 – Precious Metal Clay and Ceramics

Procedure:

1. Form, fire and glaze the ceramic item that will be embellished with silver. The silver design will require a separate firing.

2. Create the design that is to be added in silver, being sure it is appropriate in size and shape for the fired ceramic piece.

3. Transfer your design to the fired piece using carbon paper or colored transfer paper.

4. Start by outlining your design with thinned silver paste. Then complete the rest of the design within the outline. When the design is dry, add another coat of paste. Three layers will usually produce a good result. Dry the layers well between coats. If you want to create a three dimensional look in some areas, continue to build those areas up using thickened paste. When your design is complete, allow it to dry thoroughly.

5. Set the firing schedule to a slow ramp up speed of 1500°F/ 815°C per hour. This ramp up will take approximately 1 hour 6 minutes to get to the final firing temperature of to 1650°F / 900°C. Hold this temperature for 10 minutes. After holding, turn the kiln off and allow it to cool slowly to prevent thermal shock to the ceramic.

6. As always with ceramic components, ramp up slowly and allow a long time for cooling. Turn off the kiln and leave the door shut allowing it to cool to room temperature.

7. Polish the white surface of the silver with the fiberglass bristled brush and burnish or polish if desired.

8. Patina with liver of sulfur. Use a artist's brush to selectively apply the patina to certain areas or to darken some areas more than others to enhance the depth in the design.

Observations & Alternatives

As always with ceramics, you must test the compatibility of your materials. The work in this project is a stoneware tray or plate with a silky black glaze that was fired to 2291°F / 1255°C.

Finding the optimum thickness of silver paste that works on your glazes will be part of your testing. I used three layers of thin paste for the piece on this page and thickened up the high spots with more paste.

Occasionally you may encounter a problem with adherence, particularly if you are working with a non-porous glaze surface. The best results come when working with a ceramic glaze that softens or "opens up" between 1470°F/ 800°C and 1650°F / 900°C. This softened glaze promotes a strong bond between the sintered PMC and the ceramic.

If the glaze has a higher maturation temperature, simply fire the silver design onto the surface, polish the white surface of the silver with a stainless steel wire brush and continue to layer the paste. I have used many of my stoneware glazes with PMC+ and would be happy to share their formulas with you on request (see contributor information on page 94). I have also successfully used Gare Simplicity low fire glazes (www.gare.com) that fire at 1870°F / 1020°C and can be fired successfully in a PMC-Sierra programmable kiln. The only limitation for firing PMC on ceramics is the size of your kiln.

Stoneware Plate with Silver Figure

Like its ceramic clay counterpart, you can form and shape PMC at almost any point in the creative process. While it is easiest to shape PMC while it is moist and pliable, there are many techniques you can use to refine that form after the PMC is dried to either leather hard or bone-dry state. Simple carving tools are all you will need. Here's your chance to be a real "cut-up."

Chapter 6
PMC Carved and Punched

Sondra Busch "Onyx"
Photo: Rob Stegmann

Sondra Busch, "Palm Beach"
Photo: Rob Stegmann

Sondra Busch, "Sondraella"
Photo: Rob Stegmann

Chapter 6 - Precious Metal Clay Carved and Punched

*Mary Ann Devos,
"Kokopelli"
Photo: Ken Devos*

Chapter 6
PMC Carved and Punched

PMC+ Sheet is a thin, non-drying form that you can cut with craft scissors or any decorative paper punches. A traditional silversmith would require much experience and patience to create similar intricate line designs in sheet silver, cutting with a jeweler's saw. PMC+ sheet enables you to create intricate lines using deckle edge scrapbook scissors or a simple craft knife.

*Sherry Fotopoulos, "Woven Cone"
Photo: Rob Stegmann*

*Mary Ann Devos, "Dragonfly Punched"
Photo: Ken Devos*

Chapter 6 - Precious Metal Clay Carved and Punched

Carved In Silver

A Carved PMC Bead/Pendant Project
By Sondra Busch

A benefit to working with Precious Metal Clay is that is can be easily carved in the leather hard or bone-dry state. It is much more difficult to engrave solid silver and requires more expensive tools.

Materials & Equipment

PMC+ clay
PMC+ paste
Wood or cork clay

Small artist's brush
Tweezers
Rubber block
Craft knife - small
PVC roller
Carving tools
Needle files - small
Drying device
Stainless steel wire brush
Burnishing tool
Rotary tumbler with stainless steel shot
Programmable kiln
Fiberboard kiln shelf

Sondra Busch, "Palm Beach"
Photo: Rob Stegmann

Procedure:

1. We will use a cork or wood clay form as the core. (For simplicity, we will refer to this as a cork clay form.) The cork clay form must be slightly wider than your bead and needs to be symmetrical to allow the PMC bead to slide on and off easily. Keep in mind that the cork clay will remain the size you make it as it dries while your bead will be 12% smaller when it is fired.

2. Make the cork form and place it in a warm dry area to dry for at least 8 hours (or use a food dehydrator). When the piece is completely dry it will be very light and will not compress when you squeeze it.

3. Wrap a strip of paper around the cork form to measure its circumference and use this paper as guide for cutting the clay slab to the proper length.

4. Place the clear plastic sheet protector over a piece of graph paper. Roll a thick slab of clay in an elongated oval shape slightly longer than the measuring strip.

5. Cut the clay slab to the proper width for your piece using the graph paper grid below the plastic work surface as a guide.

6. Wrap a strip of paper around the cork form twice and secure the paper end with tape. This paper sleeve will allow the bead to slide on and off easily. Do not tape the paper to the cork form.

7. Wrap the PMC clay slab around the cork form, on the paper and allow the ends to overlap. If the form is not cylindrical, place the overlap on a longest section. Use a craft knife to cut through the overlap at a diagonal and use paste to join the ends. Make sure they are well attached and that you have a smooth surface.

8. Place the work in a warm dry area and allow the clay to dry on the cork form until it is leather hard. Depending upon the thickness of the clay and the level of humidity this could take 24 hours or longer. Accelerate the process using a food dehydrator.

9. Carefully remove your PMC piece from the form. It may still be damp inside where it has been against the paper. If it is, use your drying device until it is completely dry.

10. Carefully sand the edges and any rough spots on the surface and inside the piece.

11. Remove the paper from the cork form and slip your clay piece on the cork form. The PMC piece should fit snugly over the cork clay form. If it is too tight sand the cork form until the clay piece fits easily. The cork form will give the clay ring support as you carve it.

12. Use a rubber block to raise the form while you carve. Small files in different shapes will allow you to carve interesting designs into the edges of the clay. You can create surface designs with files and various carving tools.

13. When you have completed carving your design, smooth it with fine (400-600) sandpaper. Remove the PMC piece from the cork clay form and use the sandpaper again to put the finishing touch to all edges.

14. Put the bead/pendant in the programmable kiln and set the schedule to fire at 1650°F / 900°C for 10 minutes.

15. The final step is to polish first with a stainless steel wire brush. Use a burnishing tool to add accents or a rotary tumbler with mixed stainless steel shot for an overall shine.

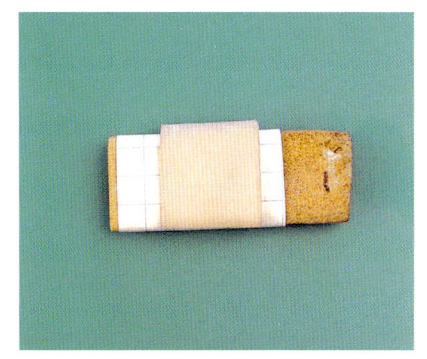

Observations & Alternatives

Carved silver pieces take on an especially attractive appearance when they are treated with liver of sulfur patina. After coloring the entire surface, bring the raised surface of the silver back to a bright finish leaving the deep carved area darker for contrast. Use consecutively finer buffing papers to produce a mirror finish on the highest areas.

Carved In Silver

Sheet Clay Pendants and Earrings

A Creative Technique using Paper Punches and Sheet Type Clay
By Sherry Fotopoulos

Sheet type clay is wonderful. It can be shaped into beautiful fabric-like folds or used to make elegant origami pieces. This is a fine weight for earrings, allowing one to make large earrings with minimal weight.

Materials & Equipment

PMC+ sheet
PMC+ paste
White glue or gum Arabic
Fine silver wire, 18-gauge
Sterling silver wire, 20 gauge

Small artist's brush
Decorative paper punches
Jeweler's pliers
Drying device
Stainless steel wire brush
Sandpaper (600 grit)
Burnishing tool
Rotary tumbler with stainless steel shot
Programmable kiln
Fiberboard kiln shelf

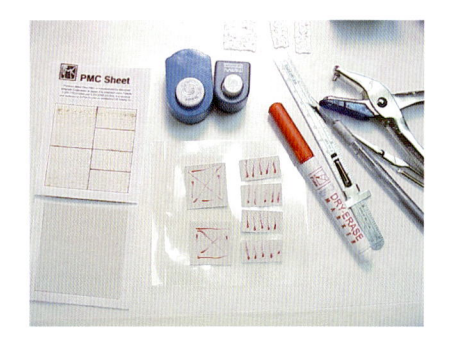

Procedure:

1. Begin by cutting the sheet in quarters. Two of the quarters will form the pendant. Then cut each of the remaining quarters into eighths of a sheet (see photo below left). Now stack the layers of sheet type clay into the earring and pendant shapes and punch out several designs with craft paper punches.

2. Separate the stacks. Turn one of the pieces in each stack 180°. This will increase the positive/negative aspects of the individual pieces and create openings that enhance the layered quality of the design. Use a light coating of white glue or gum Arabic to join these two layers. Stacking the layers enhances the design while it thickens the body of each piece to about 20-gauge (0.032" 0.80mm). This creates an extremely durable thickness for jewelry.

3. Now apply punched out design pieces using small amounts of glue and don't neglect the backside of your earrings. Be sure to correct any errors of punching too close to the edge or into another open space by applying a punched piece over the thin or empty area. If you must correct an edge, remember to apply a punched piece on the back to maintain the double-thickness of the sheet overall.

Chapter 6 - Precious Metal Clay Carved and Punched

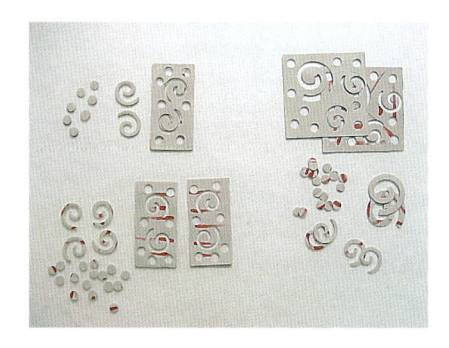

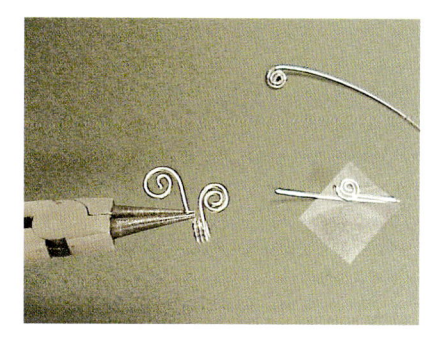

4. Cut 2 pieces of sterling silver wire 3-1/2" (8.9 cm) in length and use round nose pliers to start a coil on one end of each. These will be the earring wires. Continue shaping the coils with chain nose pliers. When the desired size coil is reached, use round nose pliers to carefully bend the wire into an ear wire shape. Begin a coil on each end of the fine silver wire and continue with chain nose pliers to desired size. Using round nose pliers, form the wire between the coils into a tight, even spring shape.

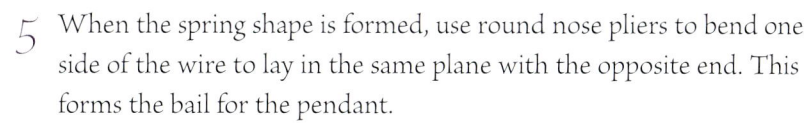

5. When the spring shape is formed, use round nose pliers to bend one side of the wire to lay in the same plane with the opposite end. This forms the bail for the pendant.

6. Attach the bail to the back of the pendant using PMC+ paste. Let dry completely, place in programmable kiln and fire at 1650°F/900°C for 10 minutes. Allow pieces to cool.

7. Use a stainless steel brush to smooth the surface of each piece, front and back.

8. If you have not left a small hole in the punched design to allow for mounting the earrings wires, use a small drill bit in a hand drill to pierce the earrings at the top.

9. Place a small piece of Liver of Sulfur in 1/2 cup hot tap water. Immerse each piece until the desired depth of color is reached. Use 600 grit (or finer) sandpaper to highlight the layers on your pieces.

10. Rinse the pieces well, then dip into alcohol (rubbing alcohol). Dry with a soft cloth. The alcohol displaces water, dries all the unreachable areas and leaves jewelry water-spot free.

11. Using a burnisher, compress the surface of selected elements to a bright shine.

12. Mount the earring pieces on the ear wires, the pendant on an appropriate chain or cord.

Sherry Fotopoulos, "Punched Pendant and Earrings" Photos: John Fotopoulos

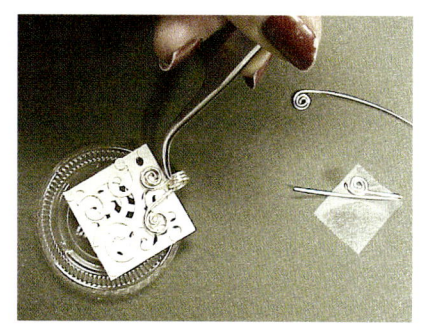

Observations & Alternatives

Planning a design on paper can be helpful but with this project one can simply jump in and have fun. The layering and positive/negative spaces add to the design and visually thicken the piece.

The PMC+ sheet has two different textures. One side is very smooth, while the side has a subtle, delicate texture. Sometimes these texture differences are irrelevant to a design. But when they do matter keep track of the different textures by marking one side of the sheet with a dry erase marker that will burn away completely during firing.

Combining other metals with silver clay has always been possible but the lower firing temperatures of PMC3 makes this process even easier. Metals such as brass, copper, sterling and steel can be intermixed successfully with PMC3.

Chapter 7
PMC and Mixed Metals

Mary Ann Devos, "Rain Dancer"
Photo: Ken Devos

Mary Ann Devos, "Corn Maiden"
Photo: Ken Devos

Mary Ann Devos, "Jester Comb"
Photo: Ken Devos

68   Chapter 7 - Precious Metal and Clay Mixed Metals

Chapter 7
PMC and Mixed Metals

These dolls allow you to put your jewelry on display when you are not wearing it.

Mary Ann Devos, "Forrest Nymph"
Photo: Ken Devos

Mary Ann Devos, "New Delhi Doll"
Photo: Ken Devos

Ken Devos, "Three Elements"
Photo: Ken Devos

Chapter 7 - Precious Metal and Clay Mixed Metals 69

Bones & Stones Necklace Pendant

Using Silver, Brass, Copper and Sterling in a Single Project
By Mary Ann Devos

Metals such as brass, copper, sterling and steel can be intermixed with PMC3 due to the low firing temperature required to sinter the silver. This opens up a world of exciting possibilities to use found objects in your work.

Materials & Equipment

PMC3 clay
PMC3 paste
PMC3 syringe
Cork clay or Plastic mask base shape
Brass, copper, sterling - assorted items
Cubic zirconia or other lab grown stones

Small artist's brush
Tweezers
PVC roller
Texture plate
Emery paper and shaping files
Drying device
Stainless steel wire brush
Burnishing tool
Rotary tumbler with stainless steel shot
Programmable kiln
Fiberboard kiln shelf

Mary Ann Devos, "Bones & Stones"
Photo: Ken Devos

Procedure:

1. Draw an image and plan to use the mixed metal item that you have.
2. Roll a medium thick slab of PMC3 clay on a slightly oiled work surface. Cut out the mask shape and move it to the face armature. This could be a dried cork form or some other domed object (see observations and alternatives on pg 71).
3. Cut out each of the additional shapes, texture them and add them with PMC3 paste to the mask (i.e. the ears and cheeks on this mask).

4. Roll a thin diameter snake coil (see page 16) and place it around the outer perimeter of the mask. The nose is a piece of the coil plus 2 small balls of clay. The mouth is a piece of copper encircled with syringe and sterling casting grains. His eyes are brass screw heads set in small balls of clay. Secure all items well with paste.

5. The headdress is made from 2 or 3 brass leaves secured to the front with clay and syringe work. Then lab-grown emerald crystals were added using syringe.

6. Use your favorite drying device to dry the piece completely (see pg 19-20). When the piece is bone-dry remove it from the form.

7. Now add the bails to the back. Use a flattened coil of clay, wrapped around drinking straws and secure with paste.

8. Thoroughly dry the piece again then use emery paper and/or needle files to refine the shape and the surface. Complete all final finishing in this dry greenware state.

9. Place the pendant in the programmable kiln and set the schedule to fire the piece at 1110°F / 600°C for 45 minutes.

10. When the piece is cooled remove it from the kiln and use a stainless steel wire brush to give your piece a matte finish and to remove the black fire scale from the brass and copper parts. It may be necessary to use fine sandpaper to remove the fire scale.

11. Use Liver of sulfur to antique the mask then highlight selected areas using a steel burnisher.

12. The pendant was incorporated into a necklace that also included stone beads from Peru, cast sterling rattlesnake bones and a hand made PMC clasp.

Observations & Alternatives

The domed base that shapes the mask can be the back of a serving spoon, the side of a drinking glass, a section of PVC pipe, a plastic bulk food scoop (as pictured at right) or just about anything that is smooth and either domed or cylindrical.

When picking the other metal objects to combine with PMC make sure that they can withstand the firing temperature. Do not use plated metals or aluminum.

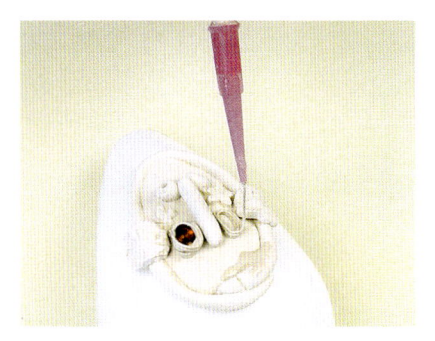

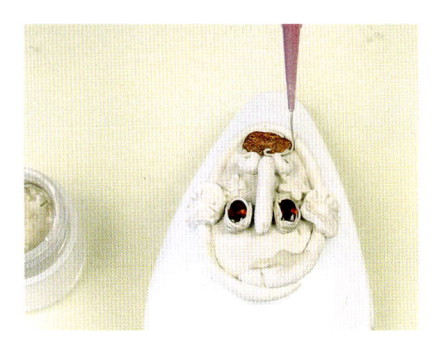

Bones & Stones Necklace Pendant

Rain Dancer Wire Figure

Sculpture Featuring a Silver Wire Armature with Slab Clay and Enamels
By Mary Ann Devos

This is a cornucopia of mixed media. I used silver clay, gold paste, enamels, assorted beads, fabric and colorful fibers. The sculptural portion of the piece is fine silver wire that combines perfectly with PMC since they are both .999 silver.

Materials & Equipment

- PMC3 clay
- PMC3 paste
- PMC3 syringe
- PMC Gold clay (made into a paste)
- 20 gauge fine silver wire
- 16 gauge fine silver wire
- Cork or wood clay
- Fiber for cloak
- Glass seed beads
- Bandage gauze

- Small artist's brush
- PVC roller
- Jewelry pliers
- Wire cutters
- Drying device
- Stainless steel wire brush
- Burnishing tool
- Rotary tumbler with stainless steel shot
- Butane torch & Fuel
- Programmable kiln
- Fiberboard kiln shelf

Mary Ann Devos, "Rain Dancer"
Photo: Ken Devos

Procedure:

1. Form cork or wood clay into a semi-round base appropriately shaped for the dancer's face or use as mask form (see page 71 Observations & Alternatives for other suggestions).

2. Roll the lump clay into a thin slab. Use a craft knife to cut the mask shape. Then add facial features and other decoration using the paste and syringe clay. Finally punch 4 holes in the lower edges of the mask. You will use these holes later to wire the mask to the body. Dry the mask completely.

3. A headpiece will be added to the top of the mask using wire and small beads. Cut 5 pieces of 20 gauge fine silver wire about 3" (7.5 cm) and attach them to the top of the mask with paste and a piece of clay to cover the inside ends of the wire. Set the mask aside to dry.

4. Next we will create the dancing body shape using 16 gauge fine silver wire. This free-form shape is easy to bend using your hands only. However you may want to use jeweler's pliers for some of the tighter bends.

5. Cut a piece of bandage gauze approximately 10" (25.4 cm) long and lay it on a plastic sheet protector. Use the artist's brush to saturate it with PMC3 paste and while it is still wet, wrap the saturated strip around the wire armature to form a shawl.

6. When you have the body shaped and wrapped the way you want it, set it aside to dry completely. When it is bone-dry use emery board and/or needle files to refine the shape and smooth the surface as desired.

7. Place the body in the programmable kiln and set the schedule to fire the piece at 1290°F / 700°C for 10 minutes, then let it cool.

8. Now we will finish the mask. Remove it from the cork form and use emery board and/or needle files to refine the shape. Then use some of the PMC gold paste to paint a few selected areas on the mask for interest. Remember to apply 2 to 4 thin coats of gold paste allowing it to dry between coats.

9. Fire the mask with the torch as directed on page 49, steps 5 & 6. When gold paste highlights are added to a bone-dry silver item it is always better to torch fired the piece for the best result.

10. When the mask is cooled, brush it with a stainless steel wire brush and tumble with mixed stainless steel shot to produce a bright shine on the silver and gold.

11. Next we will enamel selected portions of the mask using the wet pack enamel technique on page 38, steps 10 & 11. For this mask we used Thompson enamel nitric blue and peacock green. Apply the enamels and place the piece in a kiln pre-heated to 1450°F / 788°C. After 2 minutes in the kiln make a visual check of the piece to see if the enamel looks wet. If it does take it out, if not let it soak a little longer before removing. If the enamel colors are not strong enough, you can repeat the process of applying and firing thin layers until you have achieved the desired color saturation you are looking for.

12. When enameling is complete, polish the gold on the mask with a burnisher and if you wish, use liver of sulfur to apply some patina (I also antiqued the gauze shawl on the body sculpture).

13. Finish the mask by stringing beads on the headpiece wire then attach it to the head of the body sculpture with thin wire.

14. Further embellish the sculpture with beads, feathers, fabric or other items, wherever your creative heart leads you.

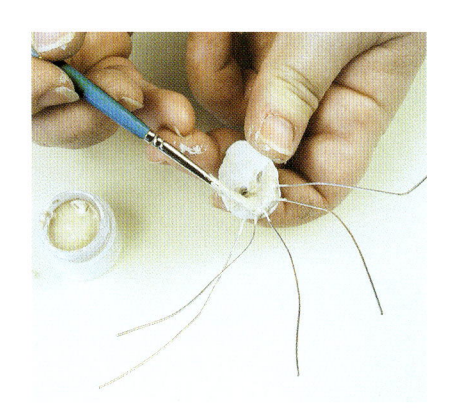

Observations & Alternatives

When sterling is subjected to high heat firing (temperatures above 1350F) it becomes brittle and more likely to fracture and we do not recommended firing sterling with PMC Standard or PMC+ clay types. However, sterling components can be successfully combined with PMC3 due to the relatively low firing temperature.

Brass or sterling will oxidize when fired with PMC3 producing a blackened metal surface referred to as 'fire-scale'. This discoloration can be removed by soaking the item in a pickle solution available from most jewelry supply outlets. This mild acid product reacts chemically with the oxides to clean the surface and remove any discoloration.

Rain Dancer Wire Figure

PMC and Chain Mail Bracelet

A combination of PMC Clay Forms and Traditional Wirework
By Ken Devos

This project employs traditional jeweler's wirework techniques combined with PMC slab clay forms. The PMC panels permit the inclusion of lab grown gemstones while the flexible fabric made of interlinked sterling silver rings (a.k.a. chain mail) provides interest and strength.

Materials & Equipment

PMC+ lump clay
PMC+ syringe
5 Cubic zirconia stones (4 to 6 mm round or oval)
20 gauge sterling jump rings (1/8" / 3.2 mm dia.)
18 gauge sterling jump rings (1/8" / 3.2 mm dia.)
18 gauge sterling wire

Small artist's brush
Tweezers
PVC roller
Texture plate
Drying device
Stainless steel wire brush
Burnishing tool
Rotary tumbler with stainless steel shot
Programmable kiln
Fiberboard kiln shelf

Ken Devos, "Blue Moon"
Photo: Ken Devos

Procedure:

1. Roll the lump clay into a thick slab (see pg 15) on a textured plate. Peel the clay slab off the plate, turn it over and place it smooth side down on the texture plate, then press to put a pattern on both sides of the clay.

2. Use a craft knife to cut 5 rectangles 5/8" x 7/8" (1.6 x 2.2 cm).

3. Use a straw to cut a light hole in each panel where you want to place a CZ. Use the PMC+ syringe without the tip and extrude a coil around one hole. Set a CZ on the extrusion bezel and press it into place (below the stones girdle). Smooth the coil using a damp paintbrush.

Repeat this process for all CZ's on all 5 panels. Decorate the panels as desired with syringe clay.

4   Punch three holes with a small plastic straw on the longer sides of the panels (6 holes per panel). These holes will be used to connect the chain mail. Place the first hole about 1/8" (3.2 mm) from the edge and equidistant from the two side edges. Place the other two holes on each edge about 1/4" (6.4 mm) away from the first hole toward the sides (see photo at right). Then dry all panels completely.

5   Smooth the edges of the panels with a sanding stick. Clean the holes.

6   Place the panels in the programmable kiln and set the schedule to fire them at 1650°F / 900°C for 10 minutes. When the panels are cool, do an initial polish with a stainless steel wire brush. Then finish a burnishing tool or place them in a rotary tumbler with stainless steel mixed shot for an overall shiny surface.

7   The chain mail will be made using 20-gauge sterling jump rings. The number you need will depend upon the length you make the bracelet (you can purchase the jump rings or make them yourself). Decide on the bracelet length, most bracelets are 7-1/2" to 8-1/2" (19 to 22 cm). Subtract 2-1/2" (6 cm) for the five panels and 1" (2.5 cm) for the clasps for a total of 3 1/2" (8.9 cm). Divide the remaining length by four to determine the length of each chain mail panel.

8   Now we will make the chain mail panels. I have fabricated a wire rack to make this process easier (see 4th photo at right). Make 12 double link chains the length you calculated in step 7. Start with two jump rings, joined by a third, then place a second ring between the first two. Continue to add jump rings to form a chain, using two rings in each segment. These chains should be an odd number of segments long.

9   When you have completed the 12 double link chains, take three and hang them next to each other on the wire rack. Take a new ring and connect the top two-ring segment of the first chain to the top two-ring segment of the second chain. Repeat the process with the second and third chains. Add a second ring to each connection. Repeat the process with the third segments of each chain and every other segment to the end. There should be about 9 segments per inch of chain. Repeat for each panel.

10 Use three 18 gauge jump rings to attach the chain mail panels to both the PMC panels and the findings (clasps). If you want to use commercial clasps I recommend sliding tube clasps, magnetically secured. Attach them to the end PMC panels using the 18 gauge jump rings. (If you want to make the clasps, the instructions follow on page 76).

11 Polish the bracelet using a rotary tumbler and stainless steel mixed shot. This will bring the bracelet to a bright shine. This also is a good way to bring it back to a high shine if it becomes dark due to wear.

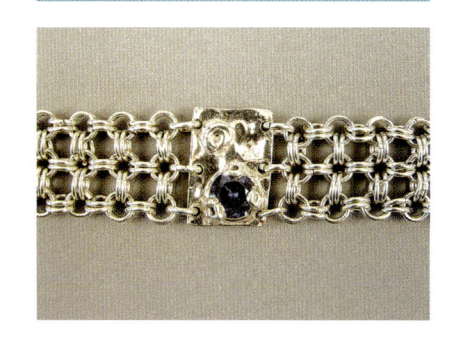

PMC and Chain Mail Bracelet

Fig 1 — Tube/dowel, Sterling wire

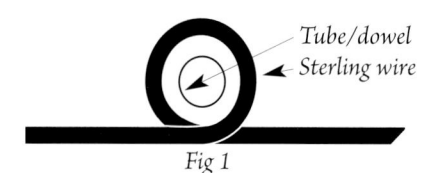

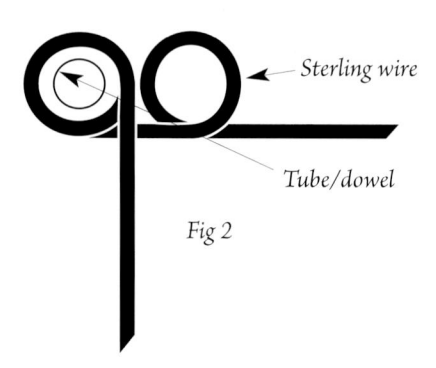

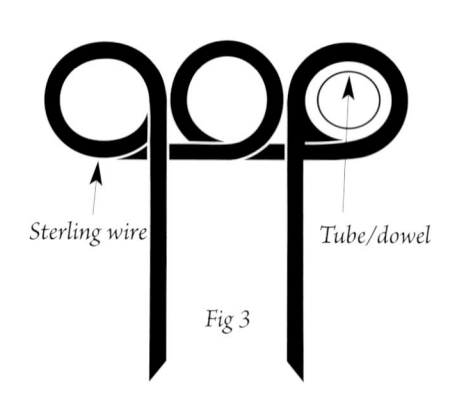

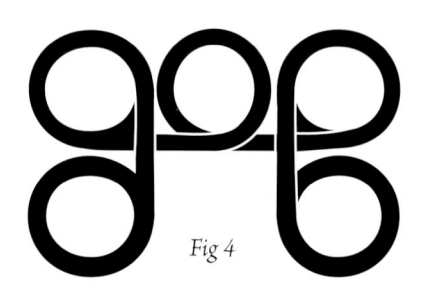

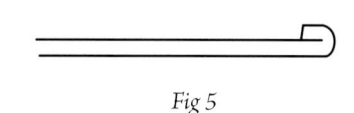

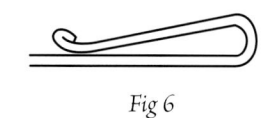

Fig 2 — Sterling wire, Tube/dowel

Fig 3 — Sterling wire, Tube/dowel

Fig 4

Fig 5

Fig 6

Clasp Instructions for Chain Mail Bracelet

The bracelet needs two clasps, a hook end and a catch end. Make these from 18-gauge sterling silver wire. Ready made sterling clasps would also work.

The Catch:

1. Cut a 3" (7.6 cm) length of 18-gauge sterling silver wire. Use a small file to smooth the ends and remove any points that were formed when the wire was cut.

2. Use a length of 1/8" (3.2 mm) diameter craft tubing (brass, copper, etc) or a wood dowel. Bend the wire in a "U" around the tube so that the ends of the wire meet evenly. Wrap the wire in a single complete loop around the tube (see fig 1). Remove the tube and place it along the wire next to the first loop. Make a second loop on the same side of the wire with the end of the wire 90° from the first loop (see fig 2). Remove the tube and repeat on the opposite side of the first loop (see fig 3).

3. Use a pair of round nose pliers to form the two ends of the wire into loops bent inward, with the ends of the wire butted against the side of the catch (see fig 4).

The Hook:

4. Cut a piece of 18-gauge sterling silver wire 3-1/2" (8.9 cm) long. Use a small file to smooth the ends and remove any points that were formed when the wire was cut.

5. Repeat the process used to make the first three loops in the catch section (figs. 1, 2 & 3).

6. Use a pair of chain nose pliers to bend the end of the wire over itself (see fig 5). Do this to the other end and make sure the bends are in the same direction.

7. Finally, use the round nose pliers and place them about half way between the loops and the end of the wire. Bend the wire around the pliers as shown in fig 6. Bend the end toward the loop until there is slightly less clearance than the diameter of the catch wire. This will insure that the hook will hold the catch when the two are joined together.

8. Attach the clasp and hook to the end PMC panels using 18 gauge jump rings.

Chapter 7 – Precious Metal Clay Mixed Metals

Fibula Pin

A combination of PMC Clay Forms and Traditional Wirework
By Ken Devos

The fibula pin is a fastener taken from ancient times. You know it as the safety pin. Our fibula pin becomes an integral part of the creative design and often contributes as much to the decoration as the pendant itself. A major benefit is, no soldering required.

1. This process requires only the most basic jewelers tools: round nose pliers, flat nose pliers, metal file, sandpaper, and polishing cloth. The materials are 16-gauge sterling silver wire and various beads and other embellishments that you may care to add.

2. Cut a 10" to 12" (25.5 to 30.5 cm) length of sterling wire. With a metal file, smooth one end of the wire and sharpen the other end into a point. Use the sandpaper and polishing cloth to smooth the pointed end. It should be smooth enough to go through cloth without snagging.

3. Using the round nose pliers, bend the blunt end of the wire to form a loop. Use the flat nose pliers to create a spiral.

4. At this point you can add beads or other items to the fibula. In fact you can add them at any point in the process.

5. With the pliers, make some patterned loops and bends in the wire next to the spiral.

6. With the flat nose pliers, bend the wire 90° from the main part of the wire, close to the area just shaped. Bend the wire 180°, doubled over about 1" from the 90° bend so that the wire returns. Make a 90° bend at the end of the doubled wire section. Use round nose pliers to bend the doubled wire over 180° to form the catch. Make the bend about 1/3 of the way from the doubled over bend (see illustration at right).

7. Add your PMC pendant to the fibula at this point.

8. At about the middle of the wire, form a series of loops over one jaw of the round nose pliers. This will form the spring to provide tension in the fibula to hold it closed in the clasp. The pliers should be held so that the loops create a form like a safety pin. The sharpened end of the wire should point toward the spiral end of the wire.

9. The pointed end of the wire should extend slightly beyond the catch element. If the end of the wire is farther than this, you can add another loop to the spring. You can adjust the size of the spring loops to adjust the positioning.

Observations & Alternatives

The fibula pin is a spontaneous creation that is never the same twice. The only critical feature is that the last 1" (2.5 cm) from the sharpened end should be straight and the very end must fit into the catch. As long as the spirals give enough spring to hold the pin in the catch you are free to create.

Fibula Pin

Precious Metal Clay is typically associated with jewelry creations. These projects are a departure from the norm as they can be described as either jewelry or sculpture depending on how they are displayed.

Chapter 8
PMC and Sculptural Forms

Mary Ann Devos, "Next Generation"
Photo: Rob Stegmann

Patti Genack, "Garden House"
Photo: Rob Stegmann

Sherry Fotopoulos, "Greek Amphoria"
Photo: Sherry Fotopoulos

78   Chapter 8 – Precious Metal Clay and Sculptural Forms

Hattie Sanderson, "His & Hers"
Photo: Hattie Sanderson

Vera Lightstone, "Crone & Child"
Photo: Rob Stegmann

Sondra Busch, "Fairy Basket"
Photo: Rob Stegmann

Chapter 8
PMC and Sculptural Forms

Hattie Sanderson, "Potion Vessel"
Photo: Hattie Sanderson

Chapter 8 - Precious Metal Clay and Sculptural Forms 79

Bird Nest Sculpture - The Next Generation
Recreating Natural Forms As Silver Miniatures
By Mary Ann Devos

Precious Metal Clay is typically associated with jewelry creations but this project could be described as either jewelry or sculpture depending on how it is displayed. It's a great place for all of us to step-out, after all there is a limit to the number of jewelry pieces a person can wear at one time.

Materials & Equipment

PMC3 clay
PMC3 paste
PMC3 syringe
Natural pearls
20 gauge silver wire
22 gauge silver wire

Small artist's brush
Drying device
Jeweler's tools, needle nose pliers, wire cutters
Stainless steel wire brush
Burnishing tool
Rotary tumbler with stainless steel shot
Programmable kiln
Fiberboard kiln shelf

Mary Ann Devos, "The Next Generation"
Photo: Rob Stegmann

Procedure:

1. The size of the nest will be established by its ultimate use. You could make a pair of tiny nests to be used as earrings or make a larger nest to become a brooch or perhaps mounted as a sculptural piece in a shadow box.

2. The basic bird's nest bowl is shaped from PMC3 lump clay, forming it like a small clay pinch pot. When the shape is just right place it (or them if making earrings) into your favorite drying device to dry the pieces completely.

3. Place a small ball of clay inside the nest, at the bottom center of the bowl shape. Cut 3 pieces of 22 gauge silver wire, 1" (25 mm) long and insert these wires into the clay ball and secure the wires with PMC3 paste. These wires will be used as the mounting prongs for the pearl eggs.

4. Use a fine tipped syringe to cover the nest with a matrix of extrusions to resemble woven grasses and twigs.

5. Depending upon the intended use, you may need to add a silver wire loop to finish an earring, a rolled coil rope for a bail, or twisted fine silver wire to hang the piece as a pendant.

6. Place the nest in your drying device to dry completely.

7. Place the nest in the programmable kiln and set the schedule to fire at 1290°F / 700°C for 10 minutes.

8. After the piece is fired and cooled, polish with a stainless steel wire brush then place it in a rotary tumbler with stainless steel mixed shot to work harden and give it an overall shine.

9. Use tweezers to position and glue the pearl 'eggs' onto the wire prongs.

10. Finish by adding earring wires, a brooch pin back, a neck chain or mount it on an interesting stand, in a gnarly twig or in a shadow box to be displayed as a sculpture.

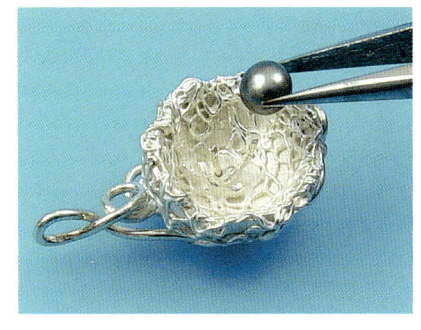

The photo above shows a black pearl. Other alternatives would be a ball of lump clay, half drilled natural stone beads, etc.

Observations & Alternatives

Natural pearls make wonderful eggs for these sculptures however there are many other possibilities such as half drilled gemstone beads or create your own eggs using PMC3 clay.

Take this sculpture one step further by creating a perfect silver tree branch to mount it on. Find a small twig that is just the right shape, coat it with PMC3 paste and fire it to burn out the core. Mount the fired nest (without the pearls) on the fired twig using paste and fire again to fuse.

This project has a fibula pin added. For instructions on this process and to see this project from the back, turn to page 77.

Mary Ann Devos, Photo: Ken Devos

Bird Nest Sculpture - The Next Generation

Silver Box with Hinged Lid

Solid Silver Containers are Great Storage for Tiny Treasures
By Patti Genack

Jewelry should not be limited to things like earrings, necklaces, bracelets, etc. These little boxes, which can be opened to store small mementoes or keepsakes, are a whimsical creation perfect for the adventurous artist looking for something unusual.

Materials & Equipment

PMC+ clay
PMC+ sheet
PMC+ paste
16 gauge silver wire
18 gauge silver wire
Cork or wood clay

Small artist's brush
Tweezers
PVC roller
Drying device
Stainless steel wire brush
Burnishing tool
Rotary tumbler with stainless steel shot
Butane torch & Fuel
Programmable kiln
Fiberboard kiln shelf

Tiny Lunchbox - frontside

Tiny Lunchbox - backside

Patti Genack, "Born With a Silver Lunchbox" Photo: Rob Stegmann

Procedure:

Create the Box Form:

1. Use cork or wood clay to create the box form. (As before, we will refer to this as a cork clay form.) This shape should be exactly as you want the box the look, including the lid shape. When you are satisfied with the shape, place the cork clay form in a warm dry area and let it dry at least 8 hours. When cork clay is completely dry it will be very light and will not compress when you squeeze it.

2 **Hinge Assembly**

We will start by creating a hinge for the box. The instructions may seem a bit complicated but after you have made one hinge it's really quite easy to do. Use one piece of PMC+ sheet clay. Cut it in half and use a glue-stick to secure these halves together to create a double thickness; set aside to dry.

3 Next we'll make the hinge pin from 16 gauge fine silver wire. Measure the back of the box, where the hinge will be installed and cut the wire to this length. Grasp the wire in a pair of forceps or tweezers and use the butane torch to melt both ends, creating small end-balls.

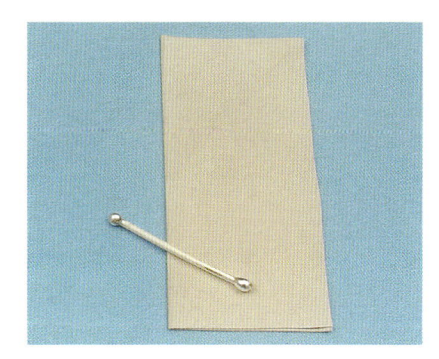

Hinge pin with melted balls on both ends

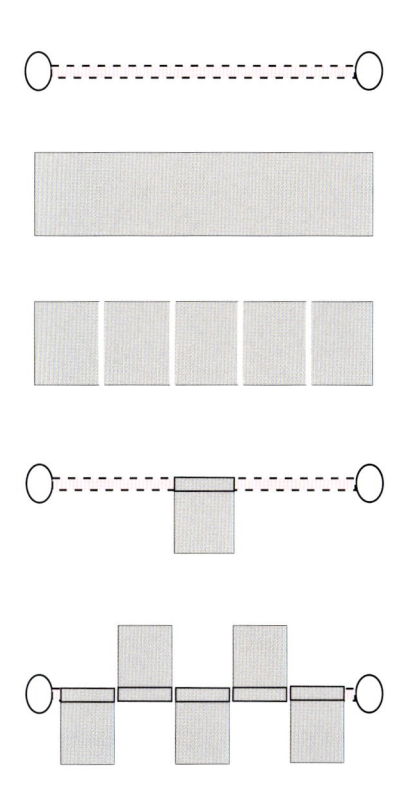

4 We need to create a spacer on the hinge pin that will burn-out during firing. Trim and use the sticky part of a Post-it™ note, wrapping it very tightly around the hinge pin, allowing the ball ends to just show beyond the paper. Two complete wraps should be sufficient. Cut away the excess and glue the paper's edge down with the glue-stick.

5 Trim the double-thick PMC+ sheet to the length of your hinge pin (just inside the ball ends) and trim the width to 5/8" (16 mm).

6 Cut the sheet into five equal sized strips (perpendicular to the hinge pin). These will become the hinges flaps.

7 Fold the end of one of the clay strips around the hinge pin allowing 1/8" (3.2 mm) to extend over and around the pin and back onto the tail of the strip. Use the glue-stick to secure this 1/8" (3.2 mm) flap back onto to clay strip (try not to glue the PMC sheet to paper). Position this hinge flap in the center of the hinge pin. Repeat the folding process with the next 2 strips, one on either side of the first, but allow these 2 flaps to extend in the opposite direction of the center flap.

8 Finally, attach the last two strips to complete both ends of the hinge. These end pieces should extend in the same direction as the center flap. Set this hinge assembly aside to let the glue dry.

Hinge pin and flaps assembly diagrams

Laminating the box:

9 Roll a medium slab of PMC+ clay. Use a texture plate if you want to give your box an interesting surface. Cut a slab section for each side of the box, using the dried cork form as your guide (make each slab slightly larger than the form).

10 Cover the cork form with the cut out clay slabs, blending the edges using paste clay to secure all joints.

11 Allow the clay to dry to leather hard. Then fill any cracks or imperfections with paste clay.

Covering the cork form with clay slabs

Silver Box with Hinged Lid

Cut completely around the circumference to separate the box lid from the box bottom. This photo shows the back side of the box where the hinge will be installed.

This is the front side of the box. The lid cut has a wavy pattern. If you try this technique be sure to only put the fancy cut on the front edge. The back side must be left straight to accommodate the hinge.

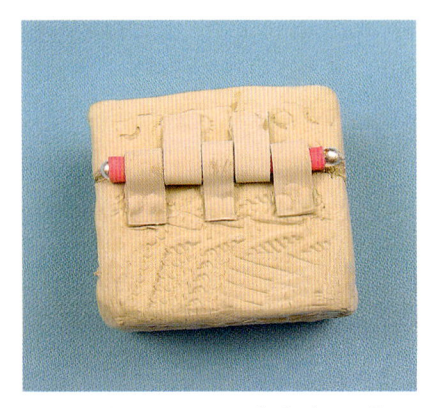

Use PMC+ paste to attach the hinge flaps to the box bottom and lid.

12 Use a craft knife to cut around and through the clay to separate the box lid from the box bottom. Make sure to cut completely around the circumference of the form and all the way through the clay layer but not too far into the cork form underneath. The cut on the side where the hinge will be placed must be straight across.

Attach the Hinge:

13 Position the hinge on the back of the box following directly along the separation seam between the bottom and the lid of the box. The number 1, 3 and 5 hinge flaps should be positioned to attach to the bottom portion of the box and the number 2 and 4 hinge flaps should be on the lid. Use PMC+ paste to attach the hinge flaps to the box bottom and lid and set the assembly aside to dry or use your favorite drying device to speed the process (see photo bottom left).

Attaching the Clasp:

14 When the hinge has dried sufficiently the next step is to install the clasp. Cut about 1" (25 mm) length of 18 gauge wire and make a small eye on each end. Bend both eye loops 90° to the shaft (see fig below).

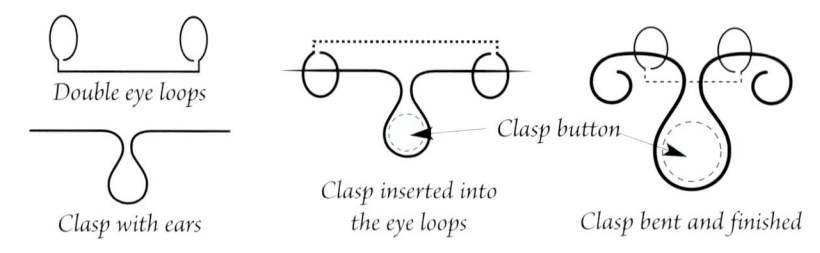

Double eye loops

Clasp with ears

Clasp inserted into the eye loops

Clasp button

Clasp bent and finished

15 Attach this eye pin to the box lid at the front center near the lip. Use a bit of paste to attach it then cover the wire between the eyes with a placket of clay. Use paste to attach a small ball of clay on the box bottom, directly below two eye loops in the lid.

Decoration and Design

16 Now you have the basic box completed. You can let your creative mind go and customize your box with inventive decorative flare. Put lettering on a slab piece and stick it to the side - like a label (see "Paris Boudoir" box on page 85), add CZ's, gold components, enamels, extrude a syringe design, create handles, and if you intend to use the box as a pendent be sure to add bails for the cord or chain.

17 When fabrication is complete, place the box in a drying device or put it in a warm dry place for several hours, until it is completely dry (see page 19-20 for dryness testing).

18 When the piece is bone-dry use emery board and/or needle files to refine the shape and smooth the surface. If cracks or blemishes have opened up, fill them with paste clay and dry again.

Firing the Box:

19. Place the dried box on a kiln shelf and put it into your programmable kiln. Fire the piece using a slow ramp-up schedule with a hold temperature of 1470°F / 800°C and the hold time at 30 minutes. A slow ramp-up schedule sets the speed of increase in temperature to 1500°F/ 816°C per hour. Note: The cork core of the box will burn off during firing and will produce some fumes. Be sure your kiln is in a well-ventilated area. The fumes are rated 'non-toxic' but it is still a good idea to avoid inhaling them anyway.

Finishing the Box:

20. Polish the fired box using a stainless steel wire brush for a matte finish, both inside and out. For a highly polished finish, place into a rotary tumbler with mixed stainless steel shot and burnishing solution.

21. Create a clasp using 18 gauge silver (or sterling) wire. Make the 'ears' of the clasp long enough to insert through the two eye pin loops in the lid and make the tongue long enough to go over the button clasp (see illustrations on page 84). This will take some bending and shaping to get it just right. The clasp should fit snugly over the clasp button and close with a snap to stay shut.

Patti Genack, "Paris Boudoir"
Photo: Rob Stegmann

This cute box opens like a purse and resembles an old-fashioned ladies boudoir case. Notice the 'Paris' sticker showing this one has been on a trip to 'the continent' with its owner.

Observations & Alternatives

Boxes and containers are fun to make. People seem to enjoy items that move and they love to have places to hide their treasures. The locket pendant is a perennial favorite 'container type' jewelry item. A locket is nothing more than a miniature flat box and could be fabricated using a method similar to the one used for this project.

The hinge described in this project is only one type that you can make. Use a little engineering creativity to dream up other possibilities.

These photos show the front and back view of the same box. Notice the hinge on the back side that allows the roof section to open. The flap on the front side is actually the clasp that opens and closes by clamping a silver bead through a hole cut in the center.

Patti Genack, "Garden House"
Photo: Rob Stegmann

Silver Box with Hinged Lid

Sculptural Rings

Use Hattie's Patties to Create an Exact Size Ring Every Time
By Hattie Sanderson

Rings are one of the most popular jewelry items that people like to make using Precious Metal Clay. However, due to the shrinkage factor of the clay, exact sizing can be difficult. This project will illustrate how to use investment mandrels called *'Hattie's Patties'* to fire the clay and achieve the perfect ring size every time.

Materials & Equipment

PMC3 lump clay
PMC3 paste
PMC3 syringe
Assorted decorative items, CZ's or Lab grown stones, fine silver or 24K gold casting grains

Small artist's brush
Wooden ring mandrel
Hattie's Pattie in the appropriate size
Drying device
Files and sandpaper
Stainless steel wire brush
Burnishing tool
Rotary tumbler with stainless steel shot
Programmable kiln
Fiberboard kiln shelf

Hattie Sanderson "Five Silver Rings"
Photo: Hattie Sanderson

Procedure:

1. Measure for the correct ring size and obtain a Hattie's Pattie that is the exact size needed for the finished ring. We are going to build the slab ring 2 sizes larger to allow for the 12% shrinkage when the PMC+ material has been fired. The ring will shrink tightly to the pattie but will go no further for an accurate size.

2. Find the spot on the wooden mandrel that corresponds to the '2 sizes larger' for the ring you're going to make. Wrap a strip of freezer paper around the ring mandrel at this spot and secure it with a bit of tape. Do not tape the paper to the mandrel.

3. Use the lump clay to roll a slab. A delicate ring needs to be at least medium thickness, a more substantial ring should be made with a thick slab. Cut a strip as wide as desired for a flat band ring.

4. Moisten the clay strip with some water on a brush before wrapping it around the paper strip on the mandrel. Overlap the ends of the clay band and cut through both layers (at a diagonal) with the craft knife. Remove both cut off ends and secure the resulting "butt-end" joint with a little paste clay. The strength of the joint will be improved by adding a bit more paste clay to the joint area.

5. Decorate your ring with syringe work, casting grains or CZ's. You can build up the top of your ring with additional pieces of fancy shaped slab clay to modify the design shape.

6. Dry the ring on the mandrel to the bone-dry clay state. We find the drying box is the best way to accelerate drying due to the circulation of the air.

7. Slide the ring, paper and all off the wooden mandrel and remove the paper from inside. Use fine grade sandpaper, emery board or files to refine the design and smooth the inside and edges.

8. Place your ring on its side on the fiberboard kiln shelf. Place the Hattie Pattie inside the ring (see 2nd photo). Put the shelf in the programmable kiln and set the schedule to fire at 1650°F / 900°C for 2 hours. This firing schedule produces the strongest ring.

9. When the ring has cooled remove the Hattie Pattie by immersing it in a container of water and crumbling it with your fingers. Scrub off any extra residue with an old toothbrush. Set the water container aside and allow the water to evaporate then discard the investment residue in the regular trash (do not pour the used solution down the drain).

Safety Tip:
Always break the pattie apart under water to avoid inhalation of the dry pattie dust. Work in a well ventilated area and wear a respirator when necessary.

10. The final step is to polish the ring with a stainless steel brush. Use a burnishing tool to add accents or a rotary tumbler with mixed stainless steel shot for an overall shine.

Build your ring on the wooden mandrel

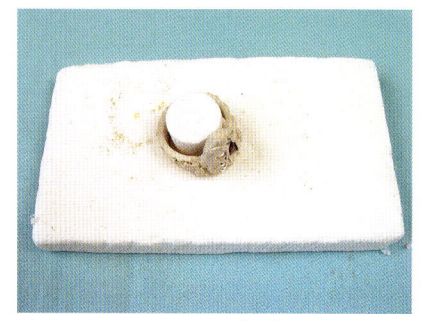

Place Hattie Pattie inside the ring

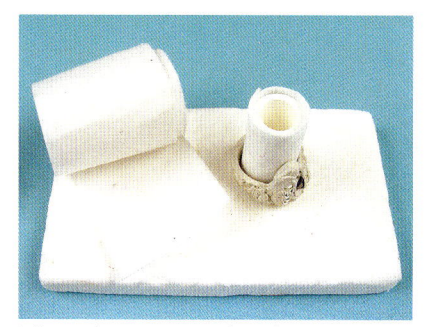

This is the same ring placed over a reusable ceramic mandrel wrapped with special firing paper for easy ring removal

Observations & Alternatives

A set of reuseable ceramic ring mandrels is available commercially that can be placed directly into the kiln with your ring in the same manner as Hatties Patties. The critical issue is to wrap the mandrel with the special firing paper provided by the ceramic mandrel manufacturer. This will enable the fired ring to easily slide off the mandrel when it has cooled.

Sculptural Rings

Turning Nature Into Silver
Building a Sculptural Design using Natural Inspiration
By Marlynda Taylor

One of the simplest yet truly amazing features of PMC is its ability to conform to intricate and complex forms and transform them into silver. This project uses an organic item as the base for a PMC sculptural piece, allowing the artist to recreate the beauty of nature in the permanence of fine silver.

Materials & Equipment

PMC+ or PMC3 lump
PMC+ or PMC3 paste
PMC+ or PMC3 syringe
Assorted organic items, e.g. leaves, dried mushrooms, seed pods, twigs, tree bark, etc.
CZ's or Lab grown stones

Small artist's brush
Drying device
Stainless steel wire brush
Burnishing tool
Rotary tumbler with stainless steel shot
Ceramic fiber blanket
Programmable kiln
Fiberboard kiln shelf

Marlynda Taylor, "Forrest Floor"
Photo: Rob Stegmann

Chapter 8 - Precious Metal Clay and Sculptural Forms

Procedure:

1. Designing pieces on the fly really gets the creative juices flowing. For a project such as this I like to choose a variety of natural dry objects that I am certain will burn away completely and safely during firing. It's important to choose some for their texture and others for their shape or for their contrasting textures. Arrange the elements you have selected in a pleasing composition. Remember that you will be using the reverse side of some items, like leaves or flower petals, so take this into consideration as you visualize your piece. As you plan your piece, consider its physical balance as well and how it will hang, looking for that strategic spot to place the hanging bail.

2. Use a separate container to mix a small amount PMC paste with enough water to make it the consistency of half and half milk. It isn't a good idea to work from your main container of paste because small bits of debris from the natural items have a tendency to get mixed into your paste. Dilute only a small amount of the paste because only the initial coat will need to be this thin.

3. Coat each element well with an initial coat of the diluted paste. This first coat captures all the fine details so be sure to get the mixture down into all of the cracks and crevices. If you chose an element for its texture, such as a leaf or a dried mushroom, coat only the most textured side. For example coat a leaf only on the underside. If you chose an element for its shape, you might want to coat both sides. Because you will be firing each element individually first, you will be able to coat some of them on only one side. Always keep in mind what will burn away and what will be captured in silver.

4. Use your favorite drying device to dry the pieces completely between coats of paste. Add successive paste coats using a thicker consistency of paste. Most items will take 3 to 6 coats while other larger or more complex shapes or textures may take 8 to 10 coats. Optimum wall thickness of a formed paste item is 1/64" (.4 mm) thick unless you are making an element that will form the foundation of your collage or will be free standing. These elements need to be 1/32" (.8 mm) thick. If you have any doubt about whether or not you have enough coats, dry the element completely. It should feel heavy for its size.

5. Some items, such as a twig, need to be coated on all sides to capture the effect however too many coats will result in a loss of texture or shape. In this case try putting only 4 to 6 coats of paste, then fire it to capture its shape and texture. You can then reinforce the element if necessary from the underside or inside and fire again.

An assortment of natural elements and components just waiting to be transformed into precious metal.

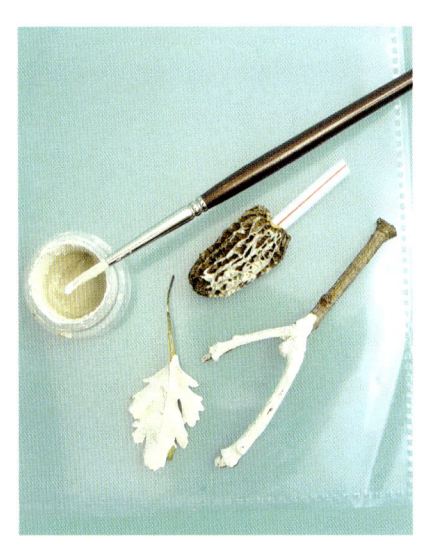

The initial thin coat is applied liberally. This first coat captures all the fine details so it is important to get the paste mixture into all of the cracks and crevices.

Turning Nature Into Silver

Leslie Tieke, "Frosted Leaf"
Photo: Rob Stegmann

6. Once all of your elements are fully coated and completely dry, place them on the ceramic fiber kiln shelf. Delicate pieces or those that may bend or collapse during firing should be supported and fired on a ceramic firing blanket. Place the shelf and items into the programmable kiln and set the schedule to fire the piece at the appropriate temperature and time for the clay type you are using. Remember, the natural core elements will burn away producing fumes and smoke, so fire the kiln in a well-ventilated area.

7. Once the elements are cooled, examine them for places that may need to be patched or reinforced with additional coats of paste. You may find that some things are too delicate or that they have split apart or cracked open. Don't panic. They can easily be patched and fired again. You might even find that the split piece, or the inside of it, is more interesting anyway. Above all, don't throw anything away. Even small bits and pieces should be saved to use later for texture. That broken or split piece may become just the thing you need to fill an empty space on another piece.

8. If you need to drill a small hole for jump rings or dangles, now is the time to do it.

9. Now recreate the interesting collage that you originally envisioned. This may actually be the most difficult part of the project. The reason this is called designing on the fly is because the design will rarely be the same as you thought is would be.

10. When you're ready to start joining elements paint some thick paste on both surfaces and stick them together. Place the joined elements into your favorite drying device and allow them to dry completely before attempting to add another element.

Assembly begins on the final sculpture.

Notes on Assembly:
I have found that PMC3 paste produces the strongest joints. Use it if it is available. If you have a particularly large gap to fill when joining two pieces together, use the PMC3 syringe.

Assembly Tip:
If you find that one element comes loose while you are trying to attach another element use a small butane torch to 'tack-fire' the joint. It only takes a few minutes because you are concentrating the flame on only one spot.

11. If you have fired each element in place with the butane torch, add the bail and any stones at this time. If you have simply pasted each element in place you should fire your completed collage in the kiln to ensure that everything stays connected well. Then add the bail and stones and fire again.

Chapter 8 - Precious Metal Clay and Sculptural Forms

Forming Bails

12. Roll a small amount of lump clay into a coil and use the roll-plate to get a uniform diameter (see page 16). Use a damp brush to moisten the coils entire surface, smoothing out any cracks or nicks while you're at it. Allow the coil to absorb all of the water to make it easier to manipulate.

13. The coil will absorb the moisture and when it is no longer shiny and it doesn't stick to you fingers it's ready. Spiral wrap the coil around a length of drinking straw or coffee stirring stick then suspend the straw in your drying device so that the clay doesn't touch anything and let it dry completely.

14. When the coil is dry, cut the whole spiral into full ring and half ring shapes. You will only need 1 or 2 for this project so store the extra in a small container or zip lock bag for future use.

Marlynda Taylor, "Pearls in a Pod"
Photo: Rob Stegmann

Finishing

15. Attach one or 2 of the half rings (or full rings depending on your piece) using PMC+ paste to the balance point of your piece and dry completely. Torch fire the bail to hold it in place or else handle the pasted piece very gently while trying to do further work on it.

16. Finish the design by adding some CZ stones or create some interesting syringe work or whatever you feel the piece needs to make it perfection. Dry and fire one last time.

17. The last step, as always is final finishing, polishing and antiquing. Use needle files to smooth any rough areas, then brush the surface with a stainless steel wire brush until is has a soft matte silver finish. Now bring out a higher shine by burnishing selected areas with a burnishing tool. Alternately, you could polish your completed piece in a tumbler with stainless steel shot.

18. Apply an antique patina using liver of sulfur. Many times the varied and brilliant colors you can achieve with this solution are just what a piece needs to emphasize its textures and shapes.

Marlynda Taylor, "Forrest Collage"
Photo: Ken Devos

Observations & Alternatives

The list of organic items that can be coated is almost inexhaustible. The only cautionary note is to use items that are totally dry and that you are certain will burn away completely and safely during firing. Here are some suggestions to get your mind thinking in the right direction, leaves, flower petals, dried mushrooms, seed pods, twigs, pasta, cereal shapes, potpourri ingredients, textured paper, fabric and almost anything found in the dried flower department of your favorite craft store. You get the idea.

Turning Nature Into Silver

Chapter 9
You've Got Questions, We've Got Answers

Q: My hollow form cork core paste covered piece split during firing. Why?

A: There are several reasons why this occurs.

First, the cork may not have been completely dry. When cork clay is dry it will be very light and will not compress when you squeeze it.

Second, the paste layers may have been too thin or uneven. Try to apply layers as evenly as possible and the piece should feel relatively heavy when finished.

Third, you may have fired the piece too hot or ramped the temperature up too quickly. We have found the slow ramp and low firing temperature work best.

Q. What is the best way to rehydrate PMC clay?

A. PMC+ and PMC3 reabsorb water more easily and completely than PMC Standard. If the clay is completely dry, crumble the dry PMC+ and PMC3 clay into small pieces and place them into a small plastic container (i.e. 35 mm film canister). Add enough water to cover the clay and let it set overnight. To make clay, remove the clay from the container and place it on a double thickness of plastic food wrap. Ball the wrap around the clay and knead the clay to insure thorough distribution of the water (no hard lumps). Open the wrap and allow the clay to dry to the desired consistency. To make paste, simply stir the clay and add enough water to bring it to the desired consistency.

It takes a little more patience to make clay than paste. Our teachers are a bunch of "paste-aholics", as you can see from the many paste projects and samples that are presented in this book.

Q. I accidentally put some PMC+ scraps into my PMC3 recycle paste jar. What do I do now?

A. It's OK to mix these two types of clay in the same container. However you must fire this mixture as if it were all PMC+ to ensure the silver is fully sintered. The same is true for both clay and paste forms where PMC+ and PMC3 are combined. Simply fire the mixed material to the PMC+ temperature.

Mary Ann Devos, "Musical Heart"
Photo: Ken Devos

Vera Lightstone, "Spiritual Eye"
Photo: Rob Stegmann

Q. Some of my PMC+ and glass creations cracked. What happened?

A. Even with the lowest temperature for PMC+ (1470°F / 800°C) the glass softens and fuses to the silver. The technical reason is non-compatible COE but all you really need to know is it causes stress in the glass that often results in a crack, either immediately or will at some point in the future. Another possible culprit is the PMC+ frame around the glass. If the frame is not secure and splits during firing it could also cause the glass to break. The solution is to always use PMC3 with glass and fire the piece at 1110°F / 600°C. This creates a jeweler's type setting that holds but does not fuse to the glass. Then there is no stress to break the glass.

Hattie Sanderson, "Pathway To The Stars"
Photo: Hattie Sanderson

Q. How do I know when to paint paste clay on only one side or on all sides of an organic form?

A. Consider what form you are creating. If you intend to make a solid piece, you only need to apply paste to the surface where the texture is the best. You paint a leaf only on the underside (back) of the leaf. You can do the same with a pod or other form, painting paste on one portion and leaving the unpainted part open. If you want an enclosed hollow form, like a flower bud or branch, paint paste around the entire surface, leaving only a small opening to vent the ash and smoke created during firing. Don't be afraid to create your work using multiple firings.

Mary Ann Devos, "Grandma's China"
Photo: Ken Devos

Q. What can I do with a fired piece I do not like?

A. Add more elements to the piece to enhance it using PMC3 clay and paste. Fire it again at 1650°F /900°C for 30 minutes to 2 hours. You also can cut the piece into small parts (using a jewelers saw) and add those parts to other new pieces as design elements. Remember that to fuse fired silver to unfired PMC you should use PMC3 fired at a higher temperature for a longer time than typical. Nothing should go to waste. Make yourself a recycle parts tray for bits and pieces and you will be surprised at the brilliant uses that will come to you.

Mary Ann Devos, "Ebb and Flow"
Photo: Rob Stegmann

Chapter 9 - You've Got Questions, We've Got Answers

Contributing Artist Instructors Bio's

All contributors to this book are PMC Connection Senior Teachers. They spend much of their time presenting PMC Guild certification classes worldwide. For information on their classes visit www.pmcconnection.com

Linda Bernstein, a polymer artist, is a veteran author, art juror and exhibit curator. Linda has also made appearances on the Carol Duvall show. She holds a BA in Art Education and a Masters in Special Education. Her artwork is available through galleries, and her website www.Artique.org

Sondra Busch, a contemporary bead artist, has owned a fine clothing boutique that included a bead-working studio and she has extensive experience in marketing. Sondra teaches both bead-working and Precious Metal Clay at her studio. Reach her at www.pmc-plus.com

Mary Ellin D'Agostino has trained and worked in pencil, pastels, oil and acrylic paints, ceramics, photography and now silver clay. She has a PhD in Anthropology. She is an award winning teacher with over 10 years of experience teaching students of all ages in a variety of academic, artistic, and physical activities. www.medacreations.com

Tonya Davidson's creative background includes contemporary ceramics, off-loom sculptural bead-work, glass fusion, lamp-worked glass, mosaics and textile design. She holds a B.S. in Interior Design and a second degree in Marketing. She has received an international award for her silver metal work. www.wholelottawhimsy.com

Sherry Fotopoulos, a sculptor and metalsmith, has an MFA in Sculpture, and has studied with international masters in Germany, Panama, and Mexico. Sherry has written two books on sculpture and many articles for art and craft magazines. Her website is www.pmc123.com

Patti Genack, a lamp-work glass artist, has 25 years experience in printmaking, painting, figurative drawing and mixed media sculpture. She is currently developing a series of pieces incorporating, combining, and intertwining hot glass with PMC. Her website is. www.whimwhambeads.com

Vera Lightstone, sculptor and potter, is a well known and respected teacher in ceramic art. Her work has been exhibited at numerous locations around the country. Her large clay and bronze sculptures have provided inspiration for her PMC pieces. Her website is www.silverclay.com

Hattie Sanderson, is a metal and fiber artist. She has a degree in Graphic Design and has had her own fine arts studio for many years where she has produced award winning works. Hattie's work has been exhibited internationally and has been published in several books.

Marlynda Taylor, mixed media with particular interest in glass fusing and organic forms. She was an English and creative writing teacher for many years. She now uses PMC as a means to give visible form to her creative vision. You can reach her through the www.pmcconnection.com website.

Leslie Tieke, a polymer and enamel artist, is known for her attention to detail in her exquisite mosaic bottle constructions and her micro-mosaic paintings. She expresses her creativity through both her artwork and her interest in ballroom dancing. You can see some of her work on her web site, www.preciousmetalclay.net

Index

A

Antique Patina 24
    Liver of sulfur 24
Art & Jewelry Galleries 25
    PMC & Bead Garden 25
    PMC & Glass 26
    PMC and Ceramics 54
    PMC and Enamel 34
        Enamel In PMC 39
        Enamel On PMC 35
    PMC and Mixed Metals 68
    PMC and Polymer Clay 42
    PMC and Sculptural Forms 78
    PMC Carved and Punched 62
    PMC Silver and 22K Gold 46

C

Contributing Artist Bio's 94

E

Embellishments and Findings 13
    Casting grains 13
    Cubic zirconia 13, 17
    Findings 13
    Fine silver wire 13
    Lab-grown gemstones 13, 18
    Natural Gemstones 13, 18

F

Format Types 8
    Lump Clay 8
    Paper Sheet 9
    Paste Clay 9
    Syringe Clay 8
Forms of PMC 6
Fundamental Techniques 15
    Coil 'Snake' Forming 16
    Drying, Refining and Firing 19, 20
    Finishing, Polishing and Antiquing 22
    Firing with Glass Inclusions 21
    Forming, Shaping and Texturing 15
    Moisture Retention and Storage 15
    Paste Coating 16
    Shaping and Texturing 17
    Slab Rolling 15
    Stone Setting With PMC 18
    Syringe Extrusion 16

I

Introduction to PMC 6

K

Kilns and Firing Equipment 10, 13
    Butane torch 14
    Firing Accessories 14
    Programmable Kilns 13

M

Messages and Bios 2
    Contributing Artist Bio's 94
    Ken Devos 4
    Mary Ann Devos 4
    Special Thanks 2

P

PMC Firing Chart 8
Product Types of PMC 6
    PMC Gold 7
    PMC Standard 6
    PMC+ 7
    PMC3 7

Q

Questions & Answers 92

S

Safety Tips 9

T

Table Of Contents 5
Tools & Forming Equipment 10
    Assembly Tools 12
    Basic Tools 11
    Burnishing and Polishing 14
    Mold Making Compounds 12
    Shaping Tools 11
    Texture Materials 12
    Tools & Forming Equipment 20, 23

Wardell
PUBLICATIONS INC

Instruction, Inspiration and Innovation for the Art Glass Communnity

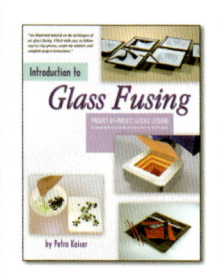

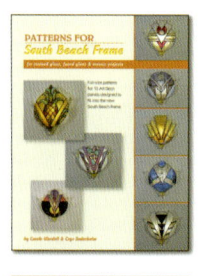

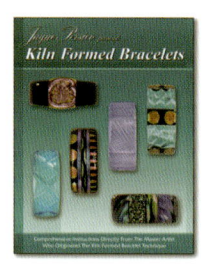

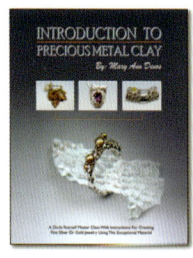

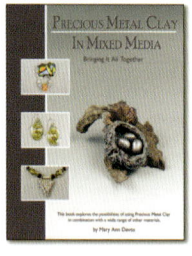

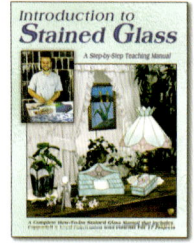

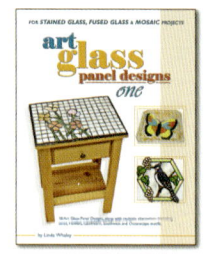

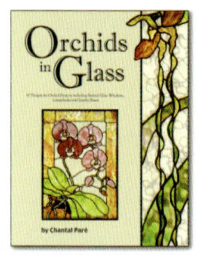

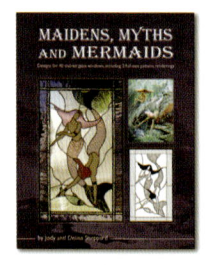

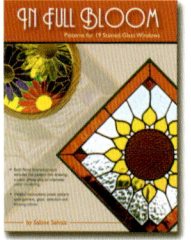

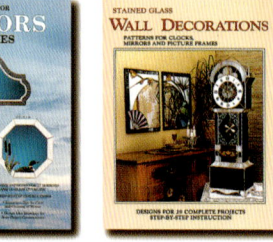

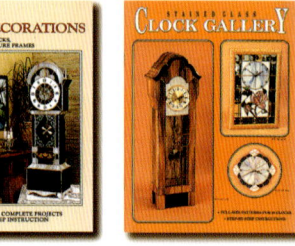

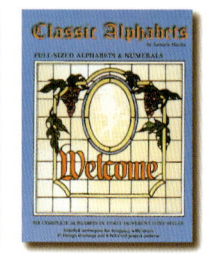

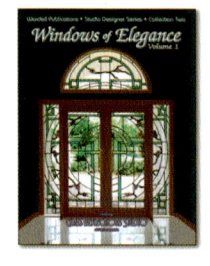

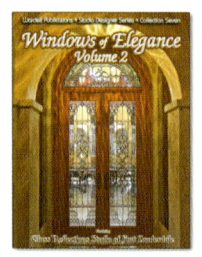

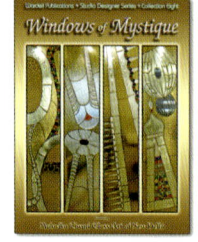

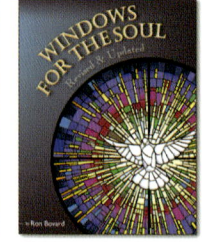

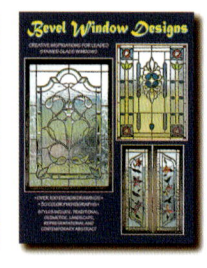

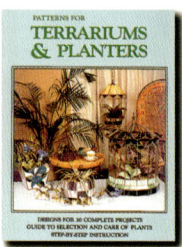

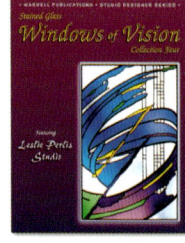

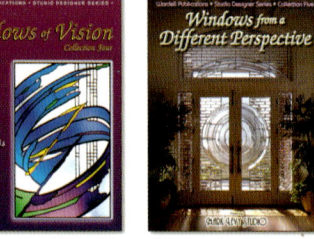

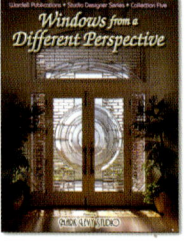

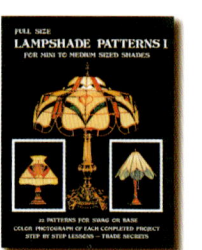

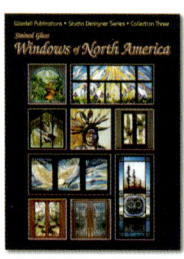

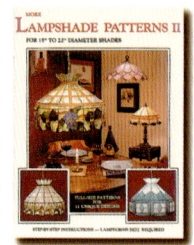

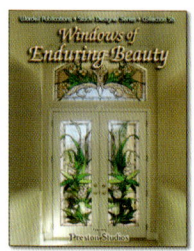

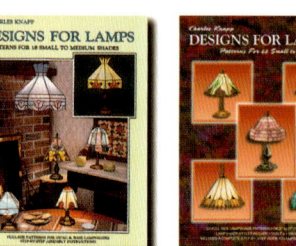

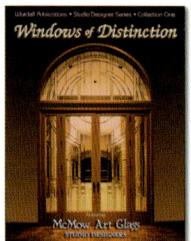

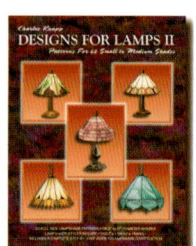

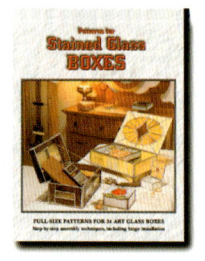

e-mail: info@wardellpublications.com   website: www.wardellpublications.com